Becky Ramsey's deliciously vibrant memoir will whisk you on an armchair pilgrimage to a tiny village in France, where, amid cobblestone streets, a gingerbread church, and a cast of quirky characters, you'll brush against the everyday sacredness of life. A delightful read filled with whimsy and charm, *The Holy Éclair* will leave you craving pain au chocolat and inspired to catch your own holy-ordinary glimpses of God.

—Michelle DeRusha, author of *Spiritual Misfit, A Memoir of Uneasy Faith,* and *Katharina and Martin Luther: The Radical Marriage of a Runaway Nun and a Renegade Monk*

Becky Ramsey's French immersion is not just one of logistics and language. She finds that the rituals of faith from her Baptist life in South Carolina simply do not translate to the heart of France. Steeped in the language of prayer and reverence, Ramsey discovers the sensuality of faith—the presence of God in painting and conversation, in letting go of "productivity," in mothering, in beauty, in apple cider, and in the perfect French éclair. Her spiritual journey is one for readers of all faiths, a revelation in the saints who surround us each day and the presence of God beyond the walls and the work of the church. But even more importantly, hers is a gentle message much needed in the conversation of spiritual shoulds and musts for today's Christian woman: that savoring God in the perfect éclair can and should be enough for one day.

—Angela Nickerson, author of *A Journey into Michelangelo's Rome*

Far from her home in South Carolina, Becky Ramsey struggled to keep her spiritual life exactly as it had always been—full of church-going, volunteerism, and Bible study. But faced with the entrancing nature of her new home in France, she wandered far afield into a land of saints and cathedrals, strong coffee and holy pastries. Becky not only awoke as a joyful Christian while in France, but also awoke as a spirited writer. *The Holy Éclair* is the rollicking story of that awakening, told in exquisite and delicious prose.

—Deb Richardson-Moore, author of *The Cover Story, The Cantaloupe Thief,* and *The Weight of Mercy: A Novice Pastor on the City Streets*

Even from the author's notes, before the book officially begins, I was captivated by Becky Ramsey's writing style, sense of humor, and above all else her relatability. So relatable, in fact, I was reminded of the great David Sedaris as Becky described the woes of navigating French pharmacies and explanations of suppositories for a sick child with vivid and hilarious detail! There is nothing holier-than-thou to be found in Ramsey's pages: you will instantly feel like you've found your new favorite friend.

—Michelle Icard, author of *Middle School Makeover: Improving the Way You and Your Child Navigate the Middle School Years*

In her new book, *The Holy Éclair*, Becky Ramsey takes the reader back to a delightful place described in her earlier book, *French by Heart*. Now, Becky invites us to return to La Belle, France and revisit people and places—and it feels good! On this visit Becky uses her ability to tell a story, describe it in detail, and then wrap it together with her brilliant sense of humor and challenging spiritual depth. As she shares her learnings from her experiences with people, situations and church, she communicates a discovery of God's presence and purpose for her life. Then, through her powerful taglines, prayers and lessons learned, Becky gives readers permission to press at our own boundaries and celebrate life where we are. *The Holy Éclair* is a gift of sweet freedom. "Take, eat!"

—Ka'thy Gore Chappell
Leadership Development Coordinator
Cooperative Baptist Fellowship of North Carolina

Every shared moment of Becky Ramsey's life is a mini memoir. Each paragraph and page is packed full of ponderings and worthy of a pause. The laughter or tears they invoke are indicative of how honestly and freely she opens her life to us. I found myself very easily connecting my celebrations and struggles to hers. The Holy Éclair is simply fun and inspiring.

—Jim Dant, Senior Pastor
First Baptist Church, Greenville, South Carolina

French By Heart:
An American Family's Adventures in La Belle France

C an a family of five from deep in the heart of Dixie find happiness smack dab in the middle of France? *French By Heart* is the story of an all-American family pulling up stakes and finding a new home in Clermont-Ferrand, a city four hours south of Paris known more for its smoke-spitting factories and car dealerships than for its location in the Auvergne, the lush heartland of France dotted with crumbling castles and sunflower fields. The Ramseys are not jet-setters; they're a regular family with big-hearted and rambunctious kids. Quickly their lives go from covered-dish suppers to smoky dinner parties with heated polemics, from being surrounded by Southern hospitality to receiving funny looks if the children play in the yard without shoes.

A charming tale with world-class characters, *French By Heart* reads like letters from your funniest friend. More than just a slice of life in France, it's a heartwarming account of a family coming of age and learning what "home sweet home" really means.

First-time author Ramsey adopts a sweet but never cloying tone to tell the charming story of her family's four-year stint in Clermont-Ferrand, France. Ramsey, a young mother of three whose husband's company relocates them to France, recounts what it feels like to sell the family home in South Carolina, say good-bye to everyone they know and move overseas. Rather than tell the story chronologically, Ramsey links the narrative to everyday events recalling the pitfalls and petite triumphs inherent in each encounter. Moreover, because the family's command of French is minimal, routine tasks often become embarrassing lessons. Ultimately, Ramsey and her family embrace their adopted country's language and customs. Entering a bookstore, she finds herself surrounded by graceful young women in high heels, short skirts and stylish leather blazers, while she is "standing there in my big red field jacket and clunky black clogs . . . like a frumpy giant." Ramsey acknowledges telling "the whole truth, even when it makes me look ridiculous"—and this results in an endearing memoir.

—*Publishers Weekly*

Travel books can generally be divided into two categories. First there are the ones in which all the traveling is done in the journey to an intended destination, at which point the writer stays put. And then there are the books in which the writer never stops—jetting, cycling, cruising, or otherwise gamboling about—often at breakneck, TGV speed.

Rebecca S. Ramsey's *French by Heart: An American Family's Adventures in La Belle France* offers no such pretensions. Unlike the flotilla of expatriates who publish memoirs of their sojourns in France, Ramsey is neither a professional writer nor an epicurean, neither an aspiring artist nor a trust-fund loafer. She's a teacher who shops at J. C. Penney and lives with her husband, a tire designer, in Kensington Farm, "a good subdivision, full of perfectly fine vinyl-sided two-story houses, with a swim team, close to the soccer fields and good schools" in Greer, S.C.

But when Michelin offers her husband a job in Clermont-Ferrand, an unremarkable industrial hub, she's game to relocate her three children for a four-year stint. "I wanted to understand it all, the Frenchness of this place," she writes. "Could we be French too, just for a little while?" Could a family of Baptists, whose children attend Vacation Bible School, survive in a land of lapsed Catholics where none of the neighbors "put wreathes on their doors or fake snow on their windows or light-up Santas or manger scenes in their yards the way people did back home"? The answer, conveyed through a series of vignette-like chapters, each wrapped up neatly like a display in the Container Store, is "Not really." A momentous tumble in a bookstore whose tall shelves are "arranged like a maze for skinny people," where Ramsey, dressed in a "big red field jacket and clunky black clogs," falls spectacularly over her rampaging toddler, comically encapsulates the reasons why.

In Ramsey's eyes, her provincial counterparts are neither categorically adorable nor absurd, despite their indecipherable mutterings and behavior. Her accounts of their prosaic routines are unexpectedly engrossing. Although she can occasionally be sentimental, the mostly genial Ramsey can also be satisfyingly snippy and droll.

—*The New York Times*

THE HOLY ÉCLAIR

Signs and Wonders from an Accidental Pilgrimage

REBECCA S. RAMSEY

© 2017
Published in the United States by Nurturing Faith Inc., Macon GA,
www.nurturingfaith.net.

Library of Congress Cataloging-in-Publication Data is available.

ISBN 978-1-63258-034-0

For my reluctant saint in flannel and combat boots,
Leah Jessie,
who always made me laugh,
especially at myself

Acknowledgments

Very special thanks to Nathan Bransford for helping me slog my way through the first messy writings and rewritings of this story, and to Jim Stewart and Kimberly Coates for their early readings and honest feedback.

Thanks to Deb Richardson-Moore, Susie Wallace, and Jim Dant for their wisdom, generosity, and encouragement.

Thanks to my editor, Jackie Riley, for making me look better than I am, and to the kind folks at Nurturing Faith for helping me share my journey.

Thanks to my mom, Judy Skaggs, for cheering me on and wrangling strangers all over the world into reading my work.

And finally, thanks to Todd and my patient, sweet family, for unveiling God to me in so many bizarre, hilarious, heart-stunning ways. You will always be my favorite ragtag saints.

Author's Note

I was still new to France the first time I held a saint card in my hands. If someone had passed it to me in South Carolina a year before, on the sidelines at soccer practice or at Wednesday night supper at First Baptist Greenville, I might have smiled, thought how strange and pretty it was—Joan of Arc with her little girl face and rosebud lips. I'm sure I would have flipped it over, commented on the novelty of it and passed it back.

But there on that August afternoon so many years ago, sitting in the sunshine on someone's patio perfumed with lilac and rosemary, the hillside before me dotted with shuttered stone houses and van Gogh cedars, I found myself strangely drawn to the Joan in my hands, just as I would soon be drawn to the Mary on the playground of École St. Pierre, my children's school, where she watched from her pedestal over lunchtime soccer matches, sometimes conveniently batting down a runaway ball with her dainty outstretched foot.

As I slipped the saint card into my wallet, between my *carte de séjour* and the ticket stub I'd saved from our final flight from Paris south to our new home in the heartland of France, I had no idea of what was about to happen to me. I'd been too busy gawking at my beautiful village, not to mention mothering Sarah, Ben, and Baby Sam; setting up house at allée des Cerisiers; and bumbling through our strange new life, hand in hand with my very own Michelin man whose job had moved us there.

But now, years later, I wonder: Did God in his humor send the Joan of Arc card my way? Was it a divine wink at what was to come? A holy hint, nudging me to open my eyes, to look for the ragtag saints and everyday wonders all around me with the same effort that I examined the man at the market selling live rabbits with bouquets of sage?

If it was a message, all I can say is "poor God." I was so clueless. I just sat there, bouncing Baby Sam on my knee and chatting with the ladies, never guessing that I was about to fall into a sacred journey, collecting along the way an entire deck of living holy cards of saints unaware who smoked and sang, who wore thigh-high boots and had dirt under their fingernails. How could I imagine that God was about to transform everyday nothings into holy signs and wonders, earning them cards as well?

I guess it was good that I didn't know. If I'd had any idea, I surely would have put down the pistachios, yanked the kids into the car, zipped back home, and fastened the shutters behind me. I loved God with all my heart, but the thought of meeting up with his errand boys was a little unnerving.

This is the story of my accidental pilgrimage out of the pew and onto the cobblestone streets of Clermont Ferrand, France. These are the sacred ordinaries and holy nobodies I encountered and tucked inside my heart for safekeeping. This is how they changed my life.

———————

Becky Ramsey is the minister to children at First Baptist Church of Greenville, South Carolina, and writes in her spare time. Her first book, French By Heart, *tells the story of her family's four years spent in a small village in central France. Her devotional work can be found in a number of magazines and in* What's a Nice God Like You Doing in a Place Like This? *She and her husband Todd are the parents of three grown children and one grandchild. To read more from Becky, visit www.beckyramsey.info.*

Chapter 1
The Saint in Pointy-Toed Shoes

At nearly eight o'clock in the evening on my fifth Friday in France, I dragged my hungry, tired family into a *pharmacie* downtown. "It'll only take a second," I promised. All I wanted was a tube of the French version of Orajel for baby Sam's gums so that I could get a decent night's sleep, but I knew I was on borrowed time. The kids had already waited a half hour in the Michelin parking lot for their daddy to finish a meeting, and everyone was teetering on the edge of a meltdown.

"What about McDonalds?" Ben and Sarah whined. "You promised!"

I hung my head in shame, praying that no one in line would understand their English. After weeks of ranting about how we are not the kind of Americans who move to France and eat at McDonalds, I had finally given in and promised them a trip as a reward for making it through their first week of French school.

"He has new teeth," I said in my best French to the skinny woman in the white lab coat, ". . . and a fever. Do you have Orajel? Something for his . . . uh . . ." I pulled back my upper lip and showed them my gums.

Why wouldn't Todd speak up? The whole reason I'd waited to visit the pharmacy was so that he could help me with the vocabulary, but the man just stood there, staring at plastic legs on the wall modeling support hose. I had to admit it: they were surprisingly sexy.

"I speak a little English," volunteered the old lady behind me. "I can help this British lady." She handed her purse to her husband, so as to free her hands, turned to me and said, "Hello," as if I were ET. She then began to explain in rapid French that the word for gums was *la gencive*, and "to teethe" was to *percer les dents*.

The pharmacist interrupted, box in hand. "Here, madame. This is for the teething pain. It's perfectly safe and will help him sleep."

The box was marked Doliprane. These were pills? How would we get a baby to swallow a pill? Crush it and put it in applesauce? Or was there a French trick to doing it?

"But do you have it in a liquid?"

"Liquid?" she said. "No, certainly not."

"But how . . . how can he . . . ?" (Not knowing the word for swallow, I demonstrated.)

The old lady gasped. The pharmacist and the assistant looked horrified. Someone standing by the bandages snickered.

"*Non, non!*" said the pair behind the counter. The pharmacist opened the package and showed me the foil wrapped pills. They were huge, too big for a baby, and tapered on one end.

Suppositories.

I am the biggest dolt in the universe.

As Ben, my first grader, twirled the rack of cough drops, Sam started yelling "Yack yack yack" in the stroller and fourth grader Sarah asked her daddy why French pharmacies don't carry candy of any kind—even those orange circus peanuts she hates—because she is starving, the pharmacist launched into a loud lecture on how to insert a suppository.

"*Oui,*" I interrupted, wishing I could ooze like a *suppositoire* right under her counter and disappear. "*Oui, je comprends* (Yes, I understand). *Suppositoires.*"

The old lady volunteered loudly, "In his azz."

"*Oui, oui,*" I said. "*Je comprends.*"

As I flipped open my wallet to pay the lady, my eyes met those of Joan of Arc. My new quirky friend Jessie had found the saint card at a flea market downtown and gave it to me as a welcome-to-France present. I had to say that I found it enchanting and more than a little weird that it seemed as if Joan had been following me around ever since our arrival.

She stared at me from atop the entrance to Lycée Jeanne D'Arc (Joan of Arc High School), waved a flag at me from a china plate in the window of the antique store on rue de Port, and even met me in a corridor at the Hôtel de Ville of Riom on a walk after a Saturday lunch with Todd's new boss and his family.

Now she accompanied me on every shopping trip, every errand out, within a photo sleeve of my wallet, like a picture of one of my children. No matter where she appeared, she seemed young but wise, gentle but strong, completely devoted to God and faithful enough to be terribly brave. Couldn't I take her example to heart?

I flipped the card over instead. Today I was too tired to be brave. No, I just wanted to snap my fingers and transform into the woman of my dreams. I hated to tell Joan, but today she wasn't my only role model, the only French saint I'd found inspiring. There was another woman.

I'd encountered her two days ago, on a morning that had started much earlier than usual. I had gotten up before the kids and taken a seat on the couch, hoping to start my day with some quiet time, but within five minutes I was in replay of what had strangely happened every single morning since our move.

I'd open my Bible and France would whisper, "Doesn't that sun feel so warm on your back? Isn't it lovely how it pours over the balcony and through the open doors?" I'd take myself out of the sunbeam and change to a hard kitchen chair, and soon I'd be focused on the birds singing or the pretty words of my neighbors chatting with each other. With all the doors to the balcony open and no screens on any windows to filter out the sound, I couldn't help but try to translate their conversation. By the time I'd finished, any prayer lingering in the back of my brain had floated like a red balloon out the open doors.

What had happened to me? The life I'd left behind in South Carolina was so orderly, so defined. Now, except for the kids' school, all my structure was out the window. I had an embarrassment of time in the most beautiful, sensual place I'd ever been, and yet my prayer life was gone with the wind.

God was waiting, listening, and I was the rude person at the party, talking to the host to be polite, but watching the guests over his shoulder.

But what guests, and what a party! My first weeks in France I was pretty sure that God had pressed the *saturate* button on earth's control panel, and suddenly the sky after dinner was purple. I couldn't understand how people were just walking around under it, buying their bread or having a smoke as they waited for the bus.

When I first heard the postman buzz his motorbike into our cul de sac, it sounded so much like an enormous bee that I stepped out on the balcony to watch him and laughed to myself as he hovered at each mailbox, as if it were a flower.

When the market set up in the center of our village, I could smell the cantaloupes and the cheese before I could even make out what they were selling. As the vendors' umbrella flaps snapped in the wind, I had the strange sensation that it was God snapping his fingers at me, saying "Hey, you with the stroller, I'm over here by the brie!"

When I tried to write just a simple prayer in my journal, the exercise bored me with such intensity that I became enthralled with the buzz of a faraway motorbike and then a rooster crowing. I had a neighbor with a rooster? Which one was that? It wasn't Madame Mallet or the Roches or Madame Fauriaux. Was it the couple on the corner, next to the man from Corsica?

I was doing it again.

By the time I waved goodbye to Todd and got everyone loaded in the car for school, I had located the rooster in question. At least that was settled.

We had to park on avenue Carnot, but I didn't mind the long walk. Ben practiced reciting *C'est la rentrée*, a poem he had down pat, though he had no idea what the words meant, and Sarah talked about the blood sausage they'd eaten yesterday as part of their regular three-course, two-hour lunch. As they talked and we walked, I steered the stroller around dog poop and up and down curbs, handed Sam his sippy cup, resisted the temptation to smile at passersby—lest they assume I was a nut or a prostitute—and thought about my unread Bible.

If I could operate this traveling three-ring circus and still keep us from being hit by a bus, why couldn't I focus when it came time for scripture or prayer? It was strange. It wasn't as if I had lost touch with God or didn't feel in tune with God or wondered where God had gone. I knew where he was: surrounding me. I felt it everywhere I went: on our walk, at the market, even here in the school courtyard as I nodded and greeted the French mommies, trying to be friendly without scaring them off.

What had changed? My busy American life full of schedules and work and purpose had now fully morphed into sunny days of leisurely chats with my neighbors, coffees with Jessie and the other expat ladies, and lazy walks through the park with my Sammy. Spending time in scripture and prayer, communing with God—not just feeling his presence—should have been a natural, easy thing to do.

But you have three kids to take care of, my workaholic inner self piped up, not wanting to appear idle—and one of them can't do much but act adorable. I ruffled Sammy's hair as he looked up at me. Was that it? Could the root of my problem really be the newfound lack of purpose in my life?

I waved goodbye to Sarah and Ben, and as I pushed the stroller out the schoolyard gate, I managed to pray a quick request: Help me find a purpose, God. And please, make it obvious.

A Peugeot honked and I looked up from Sam's stroller and saw her.

She was the most beautiful woman I had ever seen, straddling a moped and kissing a little boy goodbye.

Was someone filming a commercial? No, there were no film crews, no cameras. Everyone just walked right by her, not noticing her at all. She was in her mid-thirties like me, with wavy short brown hair like mine and sunglasses. She wore a stylish pink suit and pointy-toed heels, no stockings. She looked so French, her moped basket heaped with her helmet, a leather valise, and roses—not the long stemmed kind you find in buckets outside *la fleuriste*, but a wild, tangled, freshly cut mass. Her face glowed like that of a little girl at play.

I stood spellbound as she cupped the little boy's face in her hands and whispered into his ear. He smiled and kissed her again on both cheeks. She waved him across the street, gave him a nod, and then pursed her lips as she strapped on her helmet, climbed back onto the motorbike, and buzzed down the hill, her pretty legs glistening in the sun, her silk scarf rippling behind her in the wind, motioning me to follow.

I was no Madame Pink Suit—that was clear. Now, two days later, this little trip to the pharmacie underlined this in red, just to make sure I got it. As I pushed the stroller out the door, trailing my husband and kids like the frumpy dodo brain I felt inside, I thought of her in her pointy-toed shoes, riding away in the wind. Ever since she'd shown up on her motorbike she'd propped up her pretty legs on my brain, even hanging around for a dream the night before.

On our walk toward McDonalds, after my failure at the pharmacy, I decided to tell Todd about her.

"I had the weirdest dream."

"Tell me," Todd said, as Sarah skipped in between us and grabbed his hand.

"Mommy, Daddy, you won't believe what Madame Bioche told us about the cathedral. Did you know it's built over an ancient volcano cone? All of downtown is," she said, "and the church is right in the middle."

"What?" Ben said. "You're making that up."

"I am not. Madame Bioche said so. And before the church was there, it was a forest. People came there and worshiped trees."

"That's crazy. Who'd be dumb enough to worship a tree?"

Todd started in on an explanation of Druidism, and I put away my dream talk and laughed to myself. How perfect: the cathedral was built right over an extinct volcano cone. If my first weeks in France were any indication, this new life was going to blow sky high any spiritual routines I used to have. Hopefully they'd rain down new again.

As Ben and Sarah pressed their noses to a toy store window, I saw myself in the reflection, pursing my lips like Madame Pink Suit's. No wonder I couldn't help mimicking her. She was so elegant, happy, sexy—not self-absorbed, just the opposite: free from every bit of self-thought. She leaned forward on her bike as she took off, her scarf flying, as if to say, "Watch out, world! Here I come!

I had always imagined that I'd turn out like that, a put-together woman, oozing self-confidence, in love with the world and the world in love with me. She had zipped down the street as if nothing bad could touch her, unprotected by the steel cage of a car, unprotected from people's eyes looking her over—every bit of her—her shapely calves, her skirt fluttering in the wind, the outlines of her thighs astride the bike.

We ate upstairs at McDonalds amid a herd of loud French children running wild, swatting each other with balloons attached to plastic sticks. Their parents all sat off to the side, eating silently. The kids wolfed down their food and then joined the other children in the ball pit. Todd let Sam walk around, holding onto his hands as I finished my Royal Cheese, watched the kids having fun, and replayed the dream in my mind. I still couldn't figure it out.

In the dream we had just arrived in Clermont and were visiting Todd's boss at his home. We walked into the inner courtyard and approached the table, but instead of plates and crystal, it was set with candles—three of them. Suddenly I was alone, except for a woman sitting in a bistro chair with her back to me. She wasn't Antoine's wife, Elise; she had dark hair like mine, not blond.

She turned to face me and I realized she was the lady on the moped, Madame Pink Suit, with the silk scarf and nice legs. She looked at me with a hint of a smile and nodded at the empty seat beside her.

Should I sit down?

I heard footsteps behind me. A man's voice announced, "*Le répas est prêt.*" The feast is ready.

The camera panned back and the table vanished. The courtyard had become the cathedral, and we were standing at the altar table. An old priest stood on the opposite side, swinging a smoking box of incense back and forth, like the pendulum of a clock. There was a loaf of bread and a chalice on the table, but we weren't in the middle of a service. The three of us were all alone in the cavernous place—the priest, the woman, and me, all silent, save the creaking of the swinging chain.

The moped lady pinched off a piece of bread, grasped my hand like a child would, and pressed the bread into my palm. "Take, eat," she said. Had it been in French or English?

I looked at the bread in my hand. Should I eat it?

"Fear not," said another voice. But whose voice? Was it Joan of Arc, speaking from the saint card in my pocket . . . perhaps my own voice? I wasn't sure.

The cathedral vanished and I was standing by the pulpit in the church of my childhood. The pews were filled with friends I loved and those I'd just met—Jessie, Paige, and Cindy, Mother and Daddy, and all my aunts and uncles and cousins—lurching forward, trying to figure out if it was me or not, waiting to see what I'd do. Would I eat the bread, like Alice in Wonderland, not knowing if I'd shrink or grow or change into something else altogether?

And that was it. Sam cried out from his room in the real world and woke me up. I rubbed my eyes, trying to get my bearings. It was just a dream.

What did it mean, the woman offering the bread, and me, not eating it? My voice said to fear not, but I wasn't afraid of God. I'd spent my life running to God, not away from him. Was there something I was missing?

Thankfully Christ Church Auvergne, an Episcopal chapel offering services in English every other week, had ended its summer break and was scheduled to start up again on Sunday night. That's what I need, I thought, to get a sense of normalcy again. Of course! Church was my lifeline. It's where my people were. It's where I felt at home. Church would make everything better.

As we made our way back up the cobblestone street toward the cathedral and down again to the car, we stopped at the fountain at Place Delille to let Sarah throw in a centime. As I stood there, listening to the laughter of my children and the sound of water trickling, a man on a park bench started playing a flute, and the melody landed like a hymn on my ears.

The evening sun filtering through the trees scattered flecks of light on the children as if through a stained glass window, and suddenly the cool breeze swirled circles around all of us as if God was offering a prayer to himself for me, since I couldn't seem to offer much.

Ben wanted a centime too, and as I opened my wallet to get him a coin, my eyes met Joan's earnest ones again. You need a friend, I thought. Didn't Madame Pink Suit deserve a saint card of her own? I smiled, imagining them as sisters in God: Rose Red and Snow White.

An inner voice pulled on the reins: Hold on! You don't know a thing about her, and already you've made her a paper saint and a partner for Joan of Arc? Besides, aren't you Baptist?

I might have grown up singing "When the saints go marching in," but saints to me were people like Hope Christian (yes, that's her real name), who had spent her whole life hugging on college students who wandered into my church from the nearby campus, feeding them Krispy Kreme doughnuts and leading them in peppy hymns, like God's red-headed cheerleader. Or Topsy Cox, who had taught children's Sunday school since time began. When I was baptized at the age of ten, late by some standards, Miss Topsy stood behind the curtain, held my glasses and helped me into the water, where I would be lowered into death and raised into new life.

I laughed to myself to imagine Joan having a cup of coffee with Hope and Miss Topsy. Could they make room in the saint circle for Madame Pink Suit and her motorbike?

I knew I was rushing things but as tired as I was, she looked like love to me. And that was enough for today.

If I made her a holy card, what would it look like? Easy . . . She'd straddle her bike, her pretty legs on display, the dew still beading on her pointy-toed shoes and the roses in her basket. Of course she'd beam out a smile at the world, not one bit concerned about being taken for a nut or prostitute, her silk scarf billowing a little in the breeze, beckoning the faithful to follow. She was the patron saint of the inhibited and the frightened, people who button up their selves to hide from who they were made to be.

In big swirly lettering on the holy card I would include this tagline:

Fear not!

And the prayer on the back?

God who surrounds us, we offer you the comfortable spiritual routines we trod in day after day. Blow them sky high, to rain down new again. Give us the courage to ride through the wind as the people you made us to be.

Fear not. Wasn't that what God's messengers always said to people they met? Fear not, Rébecca. I'd have to remember that on my next trip to the pharmacie.

Chapter 2
Chez God

"It looks like a little gingerbread house," Sarah said at her first sight of our French church, "that is, if all the frosting has fallen off and mold has set in." Moments later as we settled into a pew, Sarah stretched out her hand to catch the dust drifting down from the timbered ceiling as she commented, "I think I'm going to like this ruin."

I could see what she meant by a ruin. When we'd walked down the hill to the churchyard and noticed the ivy crawling up the walls, snaking and intertwining like netting over the blotchy stucco, I'd grabbed Todd's arm and said, "Oh, doesn't it look so quaint?"

But now, as the first hymn began, I was grateful for the vines, for the natural scaffolding holding everything in place. Some of the stained glass windows had shards missing, and the rest seemed to rattle as the pump organ shook the chapel, snorting and squeezing out notes like an oversized bagpipe. Sarah and Ben clapped their hands to their ears at the sudden sound, and Baby Sam rooted into me, trying to burrow away from the racket.

As we stumbled to our feet to sing with the rest of the congregation, I looked around the pews. There was Paige and her family a few rows over and several others I had met at École St. Pierre. Cindy and her family were away for the weekend, and Jessie was nowhere to be seen. Once the singing stopped, Sam ventured out from under my armpit and settled back down on my lap, fingering the order of worship.

And then someone turned on the Flames of Hell.

The nicknamed heater was so huge that it looked like it belonged in a mechanic's garage, not in the children's corner of this Hansel and Gretel chapel. It was a jet engine, nearly drowning out the singing.

I looked at Todd and almost laughed out loud at the craziness of it all—the pump organ, the various children roaming the aisles and

calling out for juice . . . and how it could be chilly enough on a September evening to need a heater?—until I glanced back again and saw that
The Flames had begun to blaze a red-orange sheet of fire.

A couple of toddlers roamed around it like cats, scattering a box of
Legos and taking turns chewing on the chalkboard eraser. Their parents
just kept singing a few feet away. I was horrified. There was no way in
H-E-double-toothpicks that I'd let Sam crawl around back there.

Lord, a little help please? I looked to the stained glass Jesus behind
the pulpit. Even he seemed a little odd to me here, practically a toddler
himself and with curly blond hair. He eyed me skeptically, arms
outstretched, not as for an embrace but almost in a shoulder shrug, as
if to sigh, "Lady, welcome to my world. Embrace the crazy."

The chapel seemed at the same time so grim and yet cheerful—
like Eeyore with a bow on his tail—that it made me want to laugh.
The heavy blocks of gloomy dark volcanic stone framing Jesus' delicate
stained glass window, the steel pipe jutting out of the wall at an odd
angle right behind the beautifully carved wooden pulpit rising above
the pews (would the priest deliver his sermon there, like God's bird in a
cage?), the quatrefoils of stained glass in blues, yellows, and pinks, like
flower blossoms set in dreary niches of gunmetal gray . . . I stole glances
around me as everyone read from the prayer book, our voices humming
together, punctuated by the creak of the old wooden pews whenever
anyone shifted their weight.

No matter how charming or gloomy it was, I was thrilled to be
back where I could start earning my keep, teach a class, or join a
committee. Todd and I had talked about it as we got ready for church,
that though this sudden break from American busyness was a luxury,
I had to admit that I missed my work and volunteering. I scanned the
order of worship. Maybe the list of church activities was on the back. I
flipped the program over. The page was blank.

"No classes or mission projects?" I whispered to Todd, pointing to
the blank page. "Nothing?"

So much for volunteering at church . . . The children's school didn't
take volunteers either. When I tried to tell the *directrice* at École St.
Pierre that as a former teacher I'd be happy to help out, she said, "No,
madame. Our teachers are professionals and must be allowed to do

their jobs." What? Couldn't they let me put up a bulletin board or make photocopies for them? It wasn't as if I wanted to be the Joan of Arc of school or church, leading the charge for God. But couldn't I find a little grunt work to add some purpose to my life?

Besides all of that, I had to wonder how long it'd take to get used to worshiping this way. I knew I'd get used to the pump organ and the Flames of Hell—truthfully, I found it all charming and different and even fun. But could I really come to church and just sit there? Sing and pray and listen? Just show up, eat Christ's food and drink his wine, without even the smallest gift to bring?

The sanctimonious Sunday school teacher in my head put her hand on my shoulder and said, "But you bring yourself and your offering, your praise and your gratitude." Maybe, but surely I could help with something. Maybe rock the babies or start up a nursery in a corner, far away from the Flames of Hell?

Could it be that it's just what you need? I heard myself think. But I hadn't just shown up at church since I was a little girl. I knew the Baptist line that we're saved by faith and not by works, but I had to admit I liked the works. Teaching made me feel more worthy somehow, like I had done my part. I wasn't Jessie, who could just show up at church or not show up, let God slip in or out. I couldn't love God without hounding him a little. That's who I was, and I liked it that way. Joan would understand. From what I knew of her, she was all about getting things done.

There was Joan on her horse again, trotting her way into my thoughts.

When Todd had come home from work the evening of Cindy's coffee, I had shown her to him. "See, Jessie gave it to me. It's a saint card. Isn't it pretty?" Todd nodded.

"It must be a Catholic thing," I continued, "for inspiration, I guess, to honor each saint with a picture and a prayer. I don't know what it is about the card, but I can't seem to stop looking at it. I'm just in love with the little thing."

Todd took a closer look and chuckled. "Huh, I know what it is. Don't you see it? She looks just like that school picture of you from first grade—you in that little white dress. You know, the one you put on Sarah's dresser when she was a baby? Even her hair is the same."

How could I have not noticed? Looking at the girl in the gilt circle was like gazing into a tiny hand mirror of first grade me—the same haircut my mother had given me, the same hazel eyes, the little pink lips.

What a laugh! Me, a twin of the queen of bravery, Joan of Arc. Me, the scaredy cat child threatened with impeachment as president of third grade (it was during Watergate, so there you go) because I was too shy to preside. Me, the teenager who was so freaked out at the idea of speaking in front of my entire high school that I actually experienced hysterical blindness en route to the podium. The thought of me being confused with Joan of Arc was a bad joke. Todd might call me a church lady, but I was certainly no Joan of Arc. God knew that better than anyone else.

Before he handed me back the card, Todd noticed something I had missed. On the back of the card at the end of the prayer was printed, "Avec permission de l'Ordinaire."

"With permission of the . . . ordinary, right?" I said. "What do you think that means?"

"*Ordinaire* is capitalized, so it's probably a title—some kind of cleric in charge of the cards, I guess."

I was sure Todd was right, but decided I liked thinking of l'Ordinaire as another name for God, since it sure seemed that God had been whispering to me through the ordinary ever since our plane landed in France. And now, perhaps, God was at it again, speaking here in this fairytale chapel. But what was he saying?

After another passage in the prayer book, we said the Lord's Prayer in French, and I stumbled along, carefully pronouncing new words to a prayer I had known by heart for years.

"Notre Père, qui es aux cieux, Que ton nom soit sanctifié, Que ton règne vienne . . ."

I did my best at translating, to see how our versions matched up. "Our father, who is in the sky, whose name is holy, whose reign is coming . . ." I love this, I thought, moving on to the next line. I hadn't been able to concentrate on scripture since we got to France, but this I could do. Suddenly the words were fresh and full of meaning.

By the time people began to get in line for communion, Sam had drifted to sleep. Todd had tried to take him and let me get in line with everyone else, but I was glad to sit and observe this first time around. I had never lined up in the aisle to take the bread and cup while everyone watched, except once at a marriage enrichment retreat—and even then I had felt slightly embarrassed as Todd and I gave each other the elements in front of everyone. I had always loved the way First Baptist did it, allowing me the solitude of sitting in the stillness of my pew, remembering Jesus as the trays of bread (little oyster crackers, really) and juice were passed to me. We had the Lord's Supper just once a quarter to keep it meaningful, but apparently it was part of every service at Christ Church.

As Todd got in line, a boy a little older than Ben walked to the end of our pew and signaled for Ben to join him. Ben blinked puppy eyes at me. I shook my head.

"Please, Mama?"

"No, honey. You know the rule. You've not been baptized yet."

"But I'm so hungry. Look, all the other kids are going. They have real bread, and it looks so good."

"They were probably baptized as babies, sweetheart. You know Baptists don't do that. Besides, the bread should mean more than an afternoon snack."

Sarah nudged me on the other side. "I like First Baptist's tiny cups and crackers better, don't you?"

Sam woke with a start and squirmed to face me, patting my chest with both hands, wanting to nurse.

"No, Sammy, not now."

Ben whispered, "Why does the preacher wear that suit?"

"It's not a preacher in France, Ben," said Sarah. "In France it's a priest."

"Well, whatever it's called, that thing looks like it's choking his neck."

I handed Sam a toy, and he turned back around.

"Look," Ben said, nodding to the front. "They're all drinking out of the same cup! That's nasty."

"Don't call it nasty, Ben," whispered Sarah. "You'll hurt God's feelings."

Father Joe wiped the chalice with a cloth, and Sarah shook her head. "I'd hate to tell him this," she said, "but that wiping won't work.

You can wipe all you want but if you don't use soap, germs get everywhere. We could all catch a stomach bug, and if there's one thing you don't want to see in a church, it's vomit."

I shushed her and then whispered, "The alcohol in the wine probably helps kill the germs."

"It's wine?" Sarah said. "In church?"

"Ooh," Ben said. "I want some."

Todd finally ambled back to our pew. As he sat down, I looked at the end of the old bench and saw something terrifying. The pew was about to fall apart, collapsing right under us! The seat had nearly worked its way out of the side piece. I hurried us into the next row back, squeezing in beside Paige and Mike and their girls, dragging the diaper bag and the children as Sam began to wail. Couldn't we go anywhere in this country, even to a chapel full of expatriates, without making a scene?

The kids wouldn't change the subject.

"But how can they give children wine?" Sarah asked. "That's against the law in America."

"This isn't America, Sarah," said Ben. "This is France."

Todd shushed them again, and I pointed to a trio of children, taking bread and bypassing the wine. "See, they're only having bread."

Just then a little girl, no older than six, stepped up to the altar and drank from the chalice.

I didn't recognize the closing hymn, but no one else seemed to either. The entire congregation stumbled along, missing words and beats, and soon it was over.

As my extroverted husband chatted with people making their way down the aisle, I tried to do my part by straightening the blocks. Sam cruised around the children's corner, and I tried to keep an eye on him, but toddler Jesus in the window kept distracting me.

Sherry, another mom I'd met at school, must have seen me staring. "It's a little different, huh?" she said. "The plaque on the side says that the American couple who founded this chapel gave the Jesus window as a memorial after they lost their child. I've always wondered if it looks like him. I can't really see Jesus as a blond. Anyway," she smiled, "I'm glad you came. The atmosphere is a little much for some people, but I hope you'll come back."

"Oh, we'll be back," I said. Of course we would. I couldn't stay home while church went on without me. Besides, I had to hand it to Father Joe. He passed up preaching from the wooden perch to stay on the floor with the rest of us, and shared a mesmerizing sermon without a single note card. One of his statements stuck in my mind: "Our faith helps us to believe what we cannot see, and to see in this world what we believe."

I got the first part, but the second? How did my faith help me to see in this world what I believe? Right in the midst of this crazy place? With my kids chattering in the pew and Sam banging on my chest, the Flames of Hell blowing, and the pump organ blasting? See what I believe in the streets of Clermont with chocolate croissants and baguettes beckoning me to the storefront windows of *boulangeries* on every corner? God in the noise and distraction? God in the ordinary?

See it? I wasn't sure about that, and maybe I still couldn't concentrate on scripture, but I did feel God's presence more than ever before, in this chapel, in my village, at school, even in the market, as I stood with strangers and asked for my apricots. God was there then, now, and he had something to say. I could sense it, just like I could sense it when Todd stood next to me with something to say, but wanted to wait until we were alone. I could feel the same unrest and urgency in the silence. Or at least I thought I did.

For a split second I remembered Jessie that day at Cindy's house, sipping espresso in her cut-offs and combat boots. When the ladies teased her about her passion for saint cards and prayer books although she hardly ever went to church, she answered, "Hey, I love God too. I just . . . don't believe in hounding him." We laughed and she lifted her coffee cup in a mock toast to God. "For all the signs and wonders you've strewn all over France," she said, and we clinked our cups together. The ladies giggled and changed the subject, but I filed the toast away to remember. Did this church qualify as a wonder? Today it felt like one.

When I got home I couldn't quit thinking of the wonder of that place, the funny little gingerbread house with the sad patched walls and the broken windows and the pipes jutting out next to jewel box windows, the swirly wrought iron hinges on the doors and flower petals on the windows. I looked up "signs and wonders" in my concordance and found the verse from Deuteronomy, "The LORD brought us out of Egypt with a strong hand and an outstretched arm, with awesome power, and signs and wonders." If God was going to use Christ Church Auvergne as a wonder in my new French life, was there something he was trying to bring me out of?

I didn't know if there were holy cards for signs and wonders as well as saints, but this tumbledown chapel certainly deserved one of its own. I laughed to envision it. If I drew it up, I'd put Child Jesus front and center, the face of one couple's lost hope and yet the hope of our world. He'd stand, giving his shoulder shrug welcome, his curly blond hair windswept from the roar of the Flames of Hell. And in the background? The pump organ would be raising its shoulders as it sang us to life, as free-range children roamed the aisles and tendrils of ivy twisted and curled their way through the broken shards of window into the sanctuary. The card would need a prayer like every other saint card, but since I was Baptist I figured that the Ordinaire might be OK with me directing it straight to God.

And in big swirly lettering on the card I would find his note back to me:

Welcome to my world.
Embrace the crazy. Love, Jesus.

My prayer?

Lord in the sky, whose name is holy, whose reign is coming, take our broken, shabby selves, and work through us, please. Pump us back to life, filling us with your spirit. Warm us with the flames of your extravagant love.

If I had a card like that, I'd tuck it into my wallet, giving Jeanne and Madame Pink Suit a place to go when no one was looking. They could walk the aisle, sit in a pew, and if either one felt chilly she could turn on the Flames of Hell. Madame Pink Suit would bring joy and roses into the grayness, and Jeanne would get that place organized in no time—probably fix the falling-down pews and start some mission work too. Between Toddler Jesus, this lovely chapel of brokenness, and my two new saints, nothing seemed impossible. Maybe they could even work changes in me.

Lord, I'd love to be in that number when those saints came marching in.

Chapter 3
God Speaks in *Chocolat*

French people don't *faire de jogging* in public. I learned this lesson on my first (and last) run around our *quartier*, hoping to catch Madame Pink Suit's healthy glow while Todd was home for lunch with Sammy. But apparently it takes a village to train foreigners, as I was scolded by no less than three people, one of them a toddler.

First was the old lady on her balcony who stopped taking down sheets from a line stretched high across her narrow street to lean over the railing and wag her finger at me.

Next up was a man driving the smallest car I'd ever seen, his bald head enormous in the tiny window. I thought he was being kind, waving me to cross in front of him at the stop sign, but when he screeched to a stop and threw his hands in the air, I thought how pitiful I was. I don't even speak French hand signals.

At least there was a cute baby I could wave to as I ran by the bus stop on the last leg home. "*Cou cou*," I said as I approached, the standard thing French people say to their babies to make them smile. The little boy threw his pointer finger up at me like a miniature lawyer and yelled, "Non!"

That settled it. No more running in my quartier. Maybe the French did Jazzercise. I could always ask my neighbor, Madame Mallet.

As I rounded the corner she was waiting by my gate in lecture stance, feet anchored, hands free.

"My dear, this will not do," she said after shaking my hand. "I'm only sorry that I missed you before you set out in public. By the time I heard you on the driveway, Clément was standing in the way and I couldn't see what you looked like. You are not appropriately dressed, Rébecca, and the street is for cars and buses and the sidewalk for people walking. If you want to run, you must go to a track made for running.

Things must be done properly . . . with the correct attire, not in those . . . those pajamas."

So maybe these weren't the clothes God made me for, I laughed. I'd thought Madame Mallet was joking, but then I realized she wasn't. So what if I wasn't dressed as a professional athlete. Weren't black sweatpants and an old Char Grill tee shirt of Todd's acceptable running attire? "This is what Americans wear when they jog," I said. "We call them '*les* sweatpants.'"

"Call them whatever you like. It makes no difference to me. But you are in France now. It is not safe nor is it hygienic. And look at you: You are not at all well-equipped. I believe that store Decathalon at La Pardieu has clothes made for people who feel they must do that sort of thing, and I'm sure they are more attractive than this ensemble."

The next day I decided to take a power walk instead. I got to school an hour and a half before school was out, prime nap time in the stroller for Sam, and traded in my white running shoes for black lace-ups to ward off any kind of fashion intervention by the townspeople who'd hyperventilate at the sight of sneakers. So how did I end up standing in one of the nicest patisseries in town, gazing into the pastry case, ready to dive face first into puff pastry?

It was Jessie's fault.

I had just rounded the hill to the cathedral and Sam was fast asleep in the stroller when she yelled my name across Place de Victoire. I nodded and made a little wave back, hoping she'd stop. For someone who kisses at least a half dozen French cheeks every time she walks into the school gate, who throws shoulder shrugs, *bofs*, and *mon oeils* into French conversation without even thinking about it, Jessie was surprisingly oblivious to the French practice of keeping quiet in public spaces.

"Becky!" she yelled again. Didn't she see me wave? I waved again and nodded politely at the couple keeping their eyes on the crazy tall yelling woman. They weren't the only ones watching. At least a dozen people sunning themselves at a sidewalk café put down their tiny cups and cigarettes and stared. Even the Pope Urban II eyeballed her from his pedestal high atop the fountain.

Jessie didn't care.

"Can you believe it?" Jessie said, bounding toward me. "They towed my car again! I left it for what . . . ten minutes. I had to run into Marché St. Pierre for some *saucisson*, but then I got sidetracked by a fish. And when I came back, it was gone! Henri's going to kill me."

"You need a ride somewhere?"

"No. Sherry said she'd take the girls home, and Henri's going to meet me at the *prefecture*. I know what he's going to say. I can just hear him, 'We just did this last Thursday!' I'll never hear the end of it."

"Sorry. Anything I can do?"

Jessie thought a second. "You could treat me to a coffee. Would you mind? I left my wallet in my car, so I can't pay."

Why not? Sam was asleep in the stroller, so I was free as a pigeon for a *café crème* and adult conversation. Besides, this would get her off of the plaza and into a café where she could wave her arms and talk in private, hopefully at a lower volume.

Pâtisserie Antoinette was nothing like the cafés near the school we usually visited—crammed full of teenagers and old men, and clouded with secondhand smoke. At Le Salford the most you could get with your coffee was a candy bar or maybe a croissant from the boulangerie next door. This was a different world, with art deco design, roomy booths of red leather, with air that was breathable. I could imagine Madame Pink Suit slipping into one of those booths, but I guess she'd be comfortable anywhere she went.

The seats were mostly empty except for two nicely dressed ladies, sipping their coffee and talking quietly, and a man nestled in the corner, reading a paper and smoking. I followed Jessie to a booth, and a middle aged lady with a swirl of burgundy hair piled on her head like frosting on a cupcake came to take our order.

"*Un café crème, s'il vous plaît*," I said.

"That's all? Oh come on," Jessie said. "Aren't you going to have something sweet in a place like this? We never treat ourselves. This is our chance."

I laughed to myself. Jessie sure had gumption. Oh, well, if I didn't have enough cash to treat her to her standards, I could always put it on my *carte bleu*.

Jessie ordered a coffee and proclaimed that we would both have a pastry, at the same time, please, which prompted our *serveuse* to rattle off a long list of pastries I'd never heard of. Before Jessie could explain, the lady led me out of the booth to the pastry case to see for myself.

It was glorious. Behind gleaming chrome and glass were mouth-watering works of art, all lined in perfect rows on frilly papers, topped with an edible sugar oval marked in cursive Pâtisserie Antoinette. There were raspberry tartlets, with each raspberry the way God designed raspberries to be before sin entered the world, plump and unblemished; swirls of meringue and pastry cream called *pavlovas*, which looked like little volcanoes, topped with a single blueberry and a sugared violet; and *mille-feuilles*, which Americans call Napoleons, cut somehow in perfect rectangles, the icing marbled, like something out of *Gourmet* magazine. The pink and green *macarons* made my mouth water, and so did the *religieuses*, little nuns made out of double cream puffs.

It was a joy just to look at them, each a work of art, reminding me of sugary versions of the hats in the shop window by the cathedral, hats adorned with swirls or feathers, flowers and butterflies, ovals and triangles set at jaunty angles, arcs, curls, and pearls. Even my favorite, the ordinary chocolate éclair, was the model of perfection, its long perfect finger of puff pastry topped with a satin ribbon of chocolate fondant. But these éclairs were different from any I'd seen in other patisseries. Atop the fondant was a white zigzag, a pretty flourish against the dark chocolate.

Jessie chose the *tartelette au citron*.

"I'd love an éclair," I said to Jessie. "But I'll just stick with coffee. I didn't go running today."

"I do not understand," said the burgundy haired lady behind the counter, startling me with her English. "You say you did not run. Why cannot you eat an éclair?"

I was glad to switch to English. "I just meant that if I am going to eat something so rich, I should exercise. I didn't really earn it."

"*C'est ridicule*," she said. "Does the *Bon Dieu* (Good Lord) not give the sun to everyone? Or just to the ones who deserve? Who earn? Beauty is made for us, for all. Being delicious, too."

I didn't know what to say. She shrugged her shoulders at my hesitation and placed Jessie's lemon tart onto a plate. "Americans have a deep hunger, probably because they withhold. They withhold and then they

. . . What's the word? Gorge. They gorge themselves with quantity. What are you hungry for? Taste. An éclair is not so much, heh?"

What else could I do? I ordered an éclair.

She brought our coffee first. Two sugar cubes should do it. "Even the sugar cubes have style!" I said to Jessie. The paper wrappings on the pairs of cubes were decorated with famous paintings. Jessie had a Renoir, and I had a van Gogh.

Before I could drop the cubes in my tiny cup, Jessie stopped me. "I've got to show you something. Brigitte taught me yesterday how to *faire un canard.*"

Faire un canard. Do a duck?

"Here," she said, dropping a cube into her cup. It bobbed, just like a duck, and then began soaking up the coffee. Right at the moment when it was about to fall apart, lose its cubeness and become part of the coffee, she scooped it up with her spoon, popped it into her mouth, and closed her eyes, savoring the taste. I tried it too, enjoying the coffee richness just before our *serveuse* set the éclair in front of me.

"Take," she said. "Eat."

"I'll try not to gorge," I whispered to Jessie. We laughed, but as I picked up my fork, I couldn't help but play her words again in my mind. "Take, eat." Madame Pink Suit had said it in my dream, just like at church. That was weird.

"I've had éclairs before, but this is the first one I've seen with a lightning bolt on it."

"You know that's what the word éclair means, don't you?" Jessie said. "It's lightning—maybe because you want to eat it in a flash."

I took. I ate.

It was a holy moment.

Ecstasy! The velvety smoothness of the rich chocolate custard against the crispness of the puff pastry . . . How was it so light and not one bit soggy? The ribbon of fondant was shiny yet not wet, and not sugary as I expected it to be—slick dark chocolate goodness. The filling was perfection. Soon it would be gone. I slowed myself down, eating small bites. Did people know how good this was? Did Jessie?

"You should try this!" I said. "Take a bite, please?"

"No thanks. I've barely started my tart. It's good?"

"Paradise," I said, closing my eyes. It was too wonderful, the lightness, the chocolate, the cream. I replayed in my mind the scene of our serveuse offering it to me, "Take, eat," she said, as if it was Jesus' body, broken for me. It sounded ridiculous—I knew it did—to say I experienced Jesus in a chocolate éclair. But as the sun poured over us through the window and beamed off the chrome, scattering crazy rainbows all over the wallpaper, it felt like true love to me.

The coffee fumes swirled around our heads as we sat there in our precious brokenness, Jessie with her parking ticket on the table, her bag of fish and saucisson on the seat beside her, and me who had rushed her off of the place because people were looking, which was silly. Who cares if people were staring?

And then I'd thought about having to pay for her pastry, which was also silly of me, and how I hadn't gone running, which was even sillier. And then this serveuse in a pink apron pronounced that beauty and deliciousness were all made for me, whether or not I deserved it. A stranger, preaching grace to me, through pastry!

Take, eat.

Maybe it was the chocolate making me dizzy, but in that moment Pâtisserie Antoinette became a French Eden, and I had to wonder if the burgundy haired lady in the pink apron was really God in disguise, and she had planned this all out as a teachable moment, writing the truth in my soul with chocolate, because I was too hard-headed to get it any other way.

I sighed with happiness, feeling surrounded by God's goodness: in the blue, laughing eyes of Jessie across the table; in the wide circles the woman with the frosting hair made with her dishcloth while cleaning off the countertop; in the curlicues of smoke of the man enjoying his cigarette and the other booth. There was goodness and God in it all: in the glints of rainbows on the wallpaper, in the artful pastries neatly lined up, and in the lovely words I didn't understand of the two women whispering over their tea.

God was pulsing through all of it, even through the ordinary éclair I was raising to my lips, savoring in my mouth, swallowing and then remembering with a sigh of delight. God was the artist of it all, the creator of this entire blessed universe I occupied at the moment, inhabiting all these ordinary vessels for God's own enjoyment and for mine. God in the ordinaire . . . I wanted to be like that sugar cube in my coffee cup, soaking up God and the sunshine and the grace. I wanted to soak up every bit until I dissolved into it, until I became part of it—part of grace, part of God.

I took my last bite, the last taste of my lightning bolt, and a memory sparked in my mind: a zigzag of lightning in a Bible story from my childhood, the one where David calls out to God to help him as he battles his enemies and God appears on the scene, with lightning bolts flashing. I'd have to look that story up in my French Bible to see how they worded it. Would it say that out of the brightness of God's presence éclairs blazed forth? I sure hoped so.

And so the fourth holy card in my imaginary souvenir box was born, honoring the Holy Éclair, God's latest grace gift in the story of my French life. What did it look like? Front and center would be the éclair itself, of course, a perfect long finger of puff pastry topped with the velvety ribbon of fondant, finished with perfection by a zigzag lightning bolt, all cartoon style, emitting bolts of lightning in every direction.

Maybe on the card's flip side I'd draw God standing before David, with éclairs of deliciousness flashing out all around him. Or maybe it'd be Madame Pink Suit instead, holding out an éclair like a magic wand on a frilly paper. "Take, eat," she'd say.

And in big swirly lettering I'd include this tagline:

Deliciousness is made for you.

The prayer?

God, who gives the sun to everyone, thank you for grace through pastry, for coming to us in beauty and deliciousness, even when we don't deserve it. Deliver us from the dangers of withholding love in all forms. Give us each day the eyes to see you right where we are, to soak up every bit of your holiness until we dissolve into it, until we fall into your arms.

The éclair would be a nice addition to my growing stack of holy cards. I could just imagine Saint Joan and Madame Pink Suit at the altar table as the pump organ played, feeding each other grace enrobed in chocolate. God would look upon them, and as dust fell from the timbered ceiling like confectioner's sugar, God would bless it all. And in the window Jesus held out his arms, inviting others to the table.

If Ben begged for bread, he'd drive me crazy for chocolate.

Like any good thing, I had to share it, so before we left the patisserie I bought four éclairs for my sweet family. Our burgundy-headed serveuse, whose name I learned was Madame Hamon, put them in a pretty box, but before she tied it with twine I asked her to add in an extra one for me. She gave me a smile and made no mention of gorging or deep hunger.

They say lightning won't strike twice, but if it's a holy éclair from Pâtisserie Antoinette, I'd say it's worth chancing it.

Chapter 4
Bread of Life, with Chicken Feet

It wasn't my proudest moment as a disciple of Christ: Cindy knocked on the window of my parked car, scaring the bejesus—or maybe Jesus himself—out of me, and in my startled state I jerked the Bible and notebook off my lap, hiding them on the floorboard.

Why had I done that? Either I was afraid Cindy would think I was a religious fanatic, ready to hand her a tract and evangelize her, or I didn't want her seeing me slugging it out with the New Revised Standard version. Maybe it was both.

The morning had started with such promise. Sam had fallen asleep in the stroller after walking the children into school and then returning to our parking place (probably because he'd been entertaining me since 4:45 a.m.) so I could get a little studying in while he slept, even if it had to be in the driver's seat of a parked car.

This was working out fine, I thought, admiring the lovely place I had parked. The ivy on the stone wall in front of me was turning a brilliant red, a burning bush before my eyes. Maybe I would connect with God today after all and the scripture would flow along with the prayers. I slipped off my shoes onto the floor, ready to walk on holy ground.

But then I couldn't find a pen that worked. And once I did, my mind drifted in and out like it always did in France and the bottom of my left foot itched, which made me actually take off my sock and scratch, burning bush or not. I switched reading between three different passages, like turning a pillow over, trying to get comfortable.

And then Cindy appeared, revealing me to be a fraud, even if I was a Bible-toting one. I had told the ladies at drop-off that I couldn't go to coffee because I was going home to tackle a mountain of laundry that had piled up, thanks to the tininess of our French washing machine.

And yet there I sat in my car, getting nothing done.

"Sorry!" she said, eyeing the Bible on the floorboard. "I thought you were going home, but then on the way back from coffee I saw your car. I was hoping I could convince you and Sammy to go on a road trip with me this morning. I've got to find a *cocotte*. It's this French Dutch oven my mother-in-law wants me to buy for her—she says she has to have a red one—and Cecile told me about this amazing restaurant supply story a half hour down N9. But if you're busy, I'll go on by myself."

Should I go? Bible reading wasn't really working, but I wasn't lying about the laundry piles. We had finally given up on being French and hanging clothes on a line or a rack in the garage like my neighbors did. After two months of living with towels that felt like sandpaper and jeans that could be propped in the corner and impersonate the invisible man, we'd finally relented and bought a dryer.

"Why not?" I wondered, thinking maybe God could speak to me from the beautiful countryside. After all, hadn't Madame Hamon said that God had made beauty for us all? Madame Pink Suit would be all over it, though I wasn't sure what Joan would say.

"OK. Let's go."

Cindy drove, Sam slept, and I looked out the window. Overnight the cold wind and gray clouds had blown themselves south between the *puys*, the extinct volcanoes, now rounded green hills, and it was Indian summer again. The sun flooded the fields of dead sunflowers, still standing, heads bowed. The cedars spiked into the sky, and the vineyards—like the ivy on the wall—had just begun to redden a little. We passed a crumbling castle on a hill and a Mary shrine by the side of the road.

"We went to the expat church last weekend," I said.

"Oh, that's right," she said. "You never told me how it went."

"It was kind of . . . different," I said, my understatement of the year. "But nice. I looked for you. Was somebody sick?"

Cindy glanced at me with a half-smile and then turned back to the road. "No," she said, switching gears. "Actually we don't go. What can I say? We're heathens. I used to go back when it started, but then we kept going out of town and then got out of the habit. I had this women's Bible study that I loved until the leader moved back to the States. That group was church for me. But most people love it."

So Cindy didn't go to church, but she used to go to Bible study? If Bible study was important to her, how could she not go to church? Cindy was so kind and generous. It puzzled me how she eased through life, not knowing much French but laughing it all off, not feeling like she had to pretend that she knew what she was doing.

The minute we left the *autoroute*, we got lost on the country roads. As I scrambled to find our road on the map, she laughed, "Don't worry, Beck. I find the best places this way."

After a few backtracks and one U-turn so sloppy that a farmer climbed down off his tractor to shake his finger at us, we finally found the right road. A mile through a meadow we passed two donkeys mating in the sunshine. Their hee-hawing struck us so funny that we almost missed the store altogether.

The store was in the middle of nowhere, dimly lit, with lots of low shelves, like a storehouse for the Keebler elves. I rounded a corner and found myself nose to nose with a short old man carrying a live chicken under his arm. A live chicken! In the store! He wore *les bleus*, the typical blue coveralls worn by men all over France for physical labor, and his worn jacket had a squiggle of chicken poop on the shoulder. Did he let chickens perch up there?

Sam sat on the edge of his stroller, transfixed by the chicken. Until that moment he had been a baby octopus, grabbing at crepe pans and wooden spoons as I wheeled him through the store. Now he sat completely still, watching the chicken's every jerk and twitch.

"Do you like chickens, my little man?" the old man asked, lowering the chicken to Sam's eye level with a grin and thoroughly enchanting me—and making me a bit nervous at the same time. I wished he'd back up. Did chickens mind being examined so closely?

The chicken bobbed its head and scratched its claws against the man's jacket, struggling to make a break for it. It was a beautiful bird, all auburn and white, with beady eyes and bright red wattles and comb. As it darted his head, Sam looked up to me for a cue: Was this chicken good or bad?

I smiled back, pretending to be Calm Mommy—the kind of mommy who encourages her children to delight in the discovery of their natural world—not Paranoid Mommy, frozen in the aisle, envisioning a terrible chicken-toddler calamity.

This mommy conflict was my constant challenge of my life in France: Stay comfortable or risk failure? Some days I had more of Jeanne D'Arc's courage than others.

I was trying my best to venture out of my comfort zone, getting to know the French mommies at school, chatting with my neighbors or the baker in the village, venturing into the library, puzzling people by coming in the wrong door or using my pointer finger instead of my thumb to ask for one loaf of *pain de campagne*, confusing the baker into thinking that I wanted two instead of one. People were usually patient and kind and willing to try to figure out what I was trying to say. But it was nice to have a foot in the expatriate bubble too, where I might not be Madame Pink Suit, but at least I wasn't the village idiot.

Sam blabbered at the chicken, looked at me, and blabbered some more.

The man stood up and laughed, and the bird made a break for it, leaping into a nearby saucepan.

At the clatter the gray-headed woman at the counter called to him, "Arthur! You'll scare the poor baby! Control that bird, my dear!"

The man laughed to himself. "Colette, my dear," he yelled back to her, "Le Bon Dieu has given us an amazing chicken! She knows what's for dinner, and she's already trying to climb into the pan."

I was charmed with the easy banter they shared in front of me, the gratitude and good humor warming the room. Le Bon Dieu was here in our midst; as crazy as it sounds, I could feel God's presence, the Great Chef, amid the sifters and the casseroles, the saucepans and the platters, the tablecloths and the glasses.

Arthur wrestled the chicken back under his arm and tightened his hold. "Non!" he scolded the chicken, who gave him a sideways glance and stopped fighting for a moment. Then Arthur walked over to Colette to ask her something I could not hear. As they talked, the chicken did a tap dance on the countertop, making a surprise attempt to get away.

"Stop, you extraordinary chicken," he said.

"Extraordinary? I'd say ordinary. Not so ready for the pan now, heh, are you?" she chuckled and handed her husband a butcher knife.

A knife? This fairytale just turned Grimm.

"I must insist that she's extraordinary. Just wait. You'll see tonight at the table . . . ordinary maybe on the outside, extraordinary on the inside." He licked his lips, winked at me, and then turned to let himself out a side door.

As the man let himself and his chicken out, there was a flutter of wings in the sunshine and the noise of other chickens. A chicken pen was attached to the store . . . a chicken pen of death? The door closed behind him, darkening the store again.

"So," asked the woman at the counter, as she tied a tiny price tag to a miniature whisk and nodded in Sam's direction, "does he like extraordinary chickens?"

"Of course," I said, happy to be included in the joke. "And I think he likes ordinary ones too."

She nodded and peeked over the counter at Sam. "Cou cou."

Sam smiled coyly and shrunk back in his stroller.

"How old is he?" she asked.

"Eleven months," I answered.

"Does he walk yet?"

"Yes," I said, "but if he walks, he breaks everything."

It wasn't perfect French, but she understood and twirled a whisk at him with a smile.

Sam sat up straight in the stroller, perhaps wondering what other feathery creatures might pop out around the next corner. I tried not to listen for the sounds of a chicken meeting its maker, and kept shopping. The next aisle over I found an enamel bucket handpainted with fruit and wondered at how the French take the effort to make even the most ordinaire lovely. It'd be perfect in my kitchen.

As the apron lady wrapped my bucket in paper as if it were made of glass, I wondered how the store stayed in business out here, at least ten miles away from any town with a restaurant. Why had they not opened up shop in a big city or at least in the middle of a village?

I walked past a paella pan bigger than my entire stove top. France was such a crazy place. Was it considered normal for a man to take a chicken inside a store . . . to keep a chicken pen in the back and a knife under the cash register? Fresh is best, but really?

The main door opened and a twenty-something girl came in with a bare baguette under her arm and handed it to Colette, who placed it on the counter—naked bread, right on the counter where the chicken had tried to make his getaway. Sam didn't care. He started jumping up and down in his stroller at the sight of the crusty loaf.

"Are you hungry, *mon petit*?" asked Colette, picking up the baguette.

Sam reached out at the bread with both hands, still bouncing. "Maaa! Maaa!"

"No, no, Sammy. That's not yours," I said, sounding gruff, like Arthur wrestling his chicken back into control. She might not understand my words, but hopefully she got my tone. I didn't want her to assume that she could give my child any of the bread.

She opened the cash register drawer, and as I reached in my purse to pay for the bucket, the old woman moved with lightning speed, tearing off a hunk of bread and handing it to Sam. In one quick motion he brought the entire piece to his mouth and sucked on the whole thing, a smile peeking out from both sides of the bread.

The woman laughed. "Yes, my dear, take and eat. You like that, eh?" she said. "Cécile," she called to the girl who had brought in the bread, "Come see the little British boy!"

Take and eat. There it was again.

I looked at my watch as we headed home. The morning was gone, and Cindy still hadn't found her red *cocotte*. But thanks to our pair of everyday saints, Arthur and Colette, our field trip had been interesting—holy, even. I was touched that this couple had been so happy to welcome strangers into their ordinary moments and so determined to share bread with my child.

As we passed the donkeys now grazing in the field, down the twisty roads by ancient stone houses, under van Gogh swirls of sun and sky, I thought about the crusty bread, the man with his chicken, and Cindy. Is this what my French life would be? Careening through my days like a kid on *Mr. Toad's Wild Ride*, not having any idea where I'm going as surprises pop out at every turn? Was that my job now? To stand there open-mouthed, marveling at how crazy it was?

Or maybe my job was to record it; to find my own meaning in it; to draw them a card, as I had for Jeanne D'Arc, Madame Pink Suit, the church, and the éclair. Choosing the picture would be easy. There would stand Arthur and Colette, French/American gothic style: Arthur in his bleus on the right, wrangling the chicken with one hand and holding a knife with the other, his wife in her apron on the left, the baguette on the counter in front of them.

The chicken would be dancing in the air, his wattle waving back and forth, maybe with a name tag: Poulet Extraordinaire. Below the picture would be Arthur and Colette, Patron Saints of Restaurateurs, of Hungry Carnivores and Wandering Shoppers in Need of a Welcome.

And in big swirly lettering I'd include:

C'est la vie!
That's life: ordinary on the outside,
extraordinary on the inside.

And the prayer?

O God who speaks love to us through burning bushes, red-headed heathens, and old men with tap-dancing chickens, open our eyes. Give us courage to go through life like an octopus, arms outstretched, ready to grab at the bread of life the second you offer it. We know you are there in every corner, God, among the saucepans and the platters, in the fields with the donkeys, in the car as we daydream or search for you. We love you!

Nearly back to my car and my lonely little Bible, I looked back at Sam sitting in his car seat, his face still crummy from the bread. It's better not to think too much about those bird feet, I told myself. Enjoy the wild surprises that pop up in our life here as little gifts dropped from God. Hopefully they wouldn't give us salmonella.

Chapter 5

On the Wings of a Snow-White Pigeon

My first French tutoring session didn't go very well. By the end of my first hour, Baby Sam had hoisted himself onto the dining room table, stripped down to a diaper, and sat on my papers, grabbing the pencil out of my hand as Didier and I tried to conjugate first person plural of the imperfect tense of étre.

In desperation I plopped Sam down in front of a Barney videotape, which I hated doing. I had always sworn I wouldn't use the television as a babysitter, which apparently amused God. During the chaos of our packing up and moving to France, Sam had spoken his first clear words: Mama, Dada, and Rewind-y.

As Didier backed out of my driveway and drove away, my neighbor beckoned me over to her gate. "Who is that handsome man that stayed at your house for two hours and six minutes?" asked my neighbor, Madame Mallet.

"He's my French tutor," I said. "He comes once a week."

"That's good," she said. "I would teach you myself, but you clearly need someone who can explain your mistakes in your own language. Don't you think he should come more often?"

"I wish, but it is expensive."

"I'm sure it is, with him having to travel all the way from Issoire."

"Issoire?"

"Yes, you can see by the code on his license plate. You ought to find someone who lives closer. That's your lesson for today—and aren't I generous. I won't even charge you for my time!"

I thanked her with a laugh and hurried inside to start my homework. If my French didn't ever get better, Madame Mallet would be my only French friend. It was a scary prospect.

It was clear that I needed to devote some serious time to study. Besides being unable to make friends outside my little cul de sac, I was so tired of sounding like a fool every time I opened my mouth. I felt myself shrinking a little more every day, which was strange considering the almost holy connection I felt with the blooming I saw all around me. Why wasn't I blooming too?

Maybe my slow disappearing act had something to do with feeling as if my hands were tied. I missed the old, comfortable, organized way I used to serve God and the reassurance I always felt from my volunteer work, knowing I had done my part. Now I just spent my days getting splashed by God's beauty, drenched in the odd lushness of it, and yet bound from earning my keep in any way by my inability to converse.

Maybe once I could speak and act in France as I spoke and acted in South Carolina—in control, with my life nice and orderly—other things such as reading scripture without daydreaming, praying without nodding off, and ordering a rotisserie chicken without attracting an audience would naturally fall into place. At least I hoped so.

Of course that was the answer! Hadn't an unrelenting work ethic solved most of the problems in my life? Studying like a madman had always earned me A's—at least until I met Todd Ramsey and physical chemistry, all in the same semester. Hard labor and practice had vastly improved my cooking, my parenting, and even my running—well, back before I traded exercise for afternoons at the café, downing coffee and éclairs.

I had my work cut out for me. Step one? Getting rid of the half-naked Napoleon baby sitting on my dining room table—at least for two sessions a week.

Jessie suggested a childcare center in my local village. "Françoise takes Michel there and drops him off whenever she wants. It's a whole lot cheaper than you'd find back home. She says the ladies there are great with kids."

That's all I needed to know; twenty-one hours later I was standing in the village *garderie*, Sam on my hip, six inches away from the nose of a woman named Adélaïde. I stuttered out my introduction as a dozen toddlers stormed around us, distracting me with their cute baby French and grabbing each other's blankets and pacifiers.

"I only want . . . to bring Samuel a few hours a week," I tried to say as a little towheaded boy in overalls reached up and pulled off Sam's shoe, "so that I can . . . study my French with a . . . tutor."

"Yes, certainly," she said. "I see you need that."

I nodded, trying not to take offense, but she had moved on, racing through an explanation of how the system worked, what I should pack for Sam each visit, and what vaccinations were required.

"*Baa*," I said, hoping that *baa* really did mean "uh" in French. I was desperate to slow the conversation so that I could get out my question. I'd read that there was one vaccination required by the French that would give a false positive to the TB test back home.

"Ah yes, I seem to remember that from someone else years ago," she nodded. "Well, we shall not require this then."

That was easy, I thought. Then Adélaïde recited the list of signatures I would need to collect to be exempted from the vaccine. My heart sank: more French strangers to talk to.

What had happened to me? I had moved to France so thrilled that I could hardly keep still, pointing out all the gargoyles and flower markets until Ben told me I sounded like a commercial. But instead of growing into Madame Pink Suit, I seemed to be shriveling up into a shadow.

At least Sam didn't look afraid. He was especially taken with a ruddy-cheeked French girl with two sprigs of ponytails high on her head. I put him down and he toddled right after her, reaching for the rabbit dangling from her fist. The girl babbled at him, and Sam grinned at me and raised his eyebrows.

Adélaïde smiled. "See," she said, "Samuel loves it here already."

She went to find the paperwork while I sat cross-legged on the floor with the children. I smiled at the other women working with the babies, and they smiled and nodded back. I'd seen them watching me, talking to each other under their breath, but pretended I hadn't noticed. Foreigners were rare in our village.

The boy in overalls plopped down in my lap. "*Bonjour, toi,*" I said, with the same lilt as the other mommies I'd heard at school. He tilted his head and looked at me suspiciously. I smiled and he stood back up, sucking nervously on his thumb.

Adélaïde returned and handed me the papers. "Let's try thirty minutes first, just to introduce him."

"OK," I agreed, gathering Sam and the diaper bag. It'd take me a while to decipher the paperwork, but maybe we could get started next week.

Adélaïde pointed to the bag. "You can leave that. We might need it."

She wanted me to leave my bag?

"I can go now?"

"If you like . . ."

"But I haven't done the papers."

She shrugged her shoulders. "Bring it next time. You won't be gone long. Does he have a *doudou*?"

"A do-do?"

"A doudou—a special doll or blanket that he's attached to, for comfort, or a pacifier?"

"No," I said. I was his doudou. I was all he ever wanted.

I started to walk over to Sam to say goodbye, but Adélaïde wagged her finger at me and shook her head. She wanted me to leave without saying anything?

"He will be fine," she mouthed.

I wasn't so sure. But he did look happy, tumbling down the little slide and trying out the toys. And we had been there twenty minutes already. Maybe he was ready to play.

I left him.

For the next half hour I watched the clock. I walked home, which took four minutes, pushing the empty stroller in front of me like a girl playing mommy. I would have studied, but how could I concentrate? I folded three towels and put a load in the wash and thought of Adélaïde.

It was strange to call her by her first name since I didn't even know the first names of my new mommy friends at school. We all called each other Madame, which seemed to be the French way. But the formality was sometimes dropped for children, so I suppose it was appropriate for me as well. I was a child too, whether I wanted to be or not, watching the adults around me, copying their pretty words and gestures, hoping to get it right.

I made myself some coffee and then forgot it on the counter. Finally I walked back to the garderie, pushing my empty stroller, feeling a little silly as passersby peered in, looking for the baby.

Help me calm down, I said to myself—or to someone.

I was twelve minutes early, so I sat on a bench next to the boule courts. Within a couple minutes I was pacing, trying to look natural, calm.

Eight minutes later I couldn't stand it anymore. I parked my stroller by the door and walked in, only to find Sam screaming, red-faced, trying to slide out of Adélaïde's arms. She thrust him at me and he buried his face in my neck, wrapping his fingers in my hair. She shrugged her shoulders and patted his back.

"Did he cry the entire thirty minutes?" I asked.

"No," she said, "just the last twenty-eight. Let's try just five minutes next time," Adélaïde suggested. "He is very strong."

Sam wrapped himself around my neck like a mournful chimpanzee all the way home.

We stopped for a moment beside the yard with the tin-roofed shack full of pigeons. I tried to loosen Sammy's death grip. "Look at the birdies, Sammy. See?"

Sam whimpered and raised his head from under my chin to see what was making the flapping noise. The birds were walking in little orbits on the floor of the pen, cooing and pecking at the scattered seeds.

As Sam turned in my arms to get a better look, a small bird, pure white, lifted off from the floor of the pen, spreading his wings and flapping them wide at us in slow motion, as if conjuring a spell in front of our eyes. As it hovered in midair, something weird and important happened to me. For a brief moment, time stopped as the bird stared at me. It tilted its head and warbled and cooed, and as crazy as it sounds, I could feel the pulsing in its little bird body flowing into my human one, the sound stilling everything inside me. Was my heart even beating?

Finally it descended again, extending its claws to grip the chicken wire, folding in its wings. My ears opened again to the sounds around me, the cooing and warbling of the other birds, the squeak of an old man's feet on bicycle pedals as he wheeled past us, the chirp of a bird in a far-off cedar, the rattle of someone's shutters across the street.

I replayed the moment, the dove, hovering in the air, waving its wings at me as if hypnotizing me, speaking straight into my brain, my soul: This is what matters . . . stopping, seeing, hearing, breathing . . . all gifts. Let go. Leap. Untuck your wings.

This bird felt like God to me, fluttering before me like the Holy Spirit, making me sure from the inside out that these strange moments were gifts—like the fountain at Place Delille, trickling living water in my ears; the Mary statuette, opening her arms to me from her perch above the Chinese restaurant; even somehow Madame Pink Suit on her moped, her billowing scarf beckoning me like an outstretched hand.

I had to listen to these messages, even though I didn't really understand what they meant. Maybe the "let go" was about this demand I'd made on myself to perfect my French now. Why had I gotten myself in such a tizzy?

It didn't make sense to start Sam in child care at his age, right at the height of his stranger anxiety. Yes, I'd taken Ben and Sarah to Parents' Morning Out once a week when they were his age, but their caretakers spoke their language. This might stress me more than it'd help me. Besides, French kids start school at age two, so he'd begin nursery school next fall at École St. Pierre with Ben and Sarah. Maybe a friend could watch him for me, or he'd get used to Didier and me hammering it out at the table. Or maybe I'd let Barney help. Was that so terrible?

The bird kept at it, midair in the corner of my mind for some time to come, fluttering as hard as it could, hoping I'd get whatever it came to say so it could land. The Holy Spirit who prays for us when we have no words—in French or English—was right there in my face, cooing.

And the bird flutters at me still, from the face of the newest holy card in my collection—its feathers snow white, its eyes speaking into my soul.

What words would I write on the card?

> On the wings of a snow-white dove
> He sends his pure sweet love
> A sign from above
> On the wings of a dove

What prayer would I add to the card?

> Holy Spirit, sometimes we know we act like a stripped-down Napoleon baby sitting on your table, demanding to fix our problems ourselves, the way it makes sense to us, when you are right there, fluttering beside us, ready to show the way. Pull on our pigtails, Lord. Get our attention when we're lost in our own inner voices. And when we can't quiet ourselves enough to hear your voice, thank you for still being willing to let us wrap ourselves around your neck and bawl our hearts out. Be patient with us, God. Help us as we take way too long to hear your voice.

Right there in Clermont Ferrand, France, God and Dolly Parton supplied my need.

It all seems crazy but you will feel sane again, I assured myself. Yes, Sunday was just a few days away, and even though Christ Church Auvergne was a little odd, it could be my rock in all this mystery. If God could speak to me from a bird coop, I would certainly find him from my place in the pew. I just needed to find some way to contribute, to feel I was earning my keep.

In the meantime I'd try to deal with my stress and pray for acceptance of my childlike state, at least until my French got better. I might be thirty-four years old, but until I could speak like an adult, I'd be treated like just another child in France. When the day went well, I could thank God. And when it didn't, I'd have to learn to deal with it. Life moved on, and there was no rewind-y.

Chapter 6
First Eden, Then Church

A half hour into our second worship service at Christ Church Auvergne, someone's two-year-old crawled under our pew, slipped off my dangling right shoe, and tickled my foot.

I let out a yelp and tried to cover it with a cough, but thanks to the pump organ wheezing out the first verse of "Nearer, My God, to Thee," nobody seemed to notice.

The song choice was a little ironic. I'd always felt God's presence at church—sometimes it would take a few minutes, long enough for me to settle my things and my thoughts, but once I focused on the singing and the prayers God's peace always returned to me. But today . . . ? It wasn't happening. I could feel God clinging to me in the craziness of the rest of our weekend, but couldn't I sense him at Sunday night church?

My thoughts drifted back to the street scene we encountered, playing tourist that very morning in the village of Saint Saturnin. The plan was to visit the thirteenth-century château in the middle of town, but when we popped the trunk and saw that we left the baby backpack at home, we had to scratch that. Our baby octopus unrestrained could fray the nerves of everyone around him, especially mine.

Ben and Sarah were not happy with the change in plans. But just as they began stomping around, wailing about their baby brother spoiling their life, we turned the corner and saw the strangest sight we'd ever seen in France.

Pulled up beside the château was a car completely heaped with plant life. Cornstalks covered the trunk, the leaves wilted and yellowed, dirt clods still dangling from the roots, and there were thorny branches laden with raspberries all over the hood, bees buzzing around them, the juice fermenting on the paint job. Huge sunflowers baked on the windshield as birds swooped down to peck at the heads. There were wildflowers threaded through twine on the roof and dahlias the size of my fist, all wilting in the sun. How extravagant and stunning, and yet such a mess! Still, in its imperfection it was somehow . . . perfect. We walked circles around it, wondering what it was.

"Do you hear that?" Sarah said at the music in the distance. "I know that song!" We followed it around the corner and found the village church. "It's 'Sing Alleluia to Our God,'" she said. "We used to sing it at day camp."

We peered into the open doors to find a wedding in progress. The bride and groom stood at the front with the priest, and the ladies in the pews were wearing fairytale hats with huge bows, feathers, and netting. One sported a flurry of silk butterflies, and another seemed to be topped with a swirl of foamy meringue. I grabbed Todd's hand. "Can you believe it? It's like a dream."

"I know," he whispered, squeezing my hand. We led the kids away. "That car must be for the bride and groom. A little different from the shaving cream on your dad's Buick, huh?"

I laughed. "It's like a fairytale, and we get to walk around in it."

A mother cat sat at the top of a small hill, watching kittens hunting in the overgrown grass as we walked past. One of them walked up to meet us, a live shrew in its mouth, still wiggling.

"Gross!" Sarah said, inching forward for a better look.

Ben knelt before it. "You're a good hunter, aren't you?" he said. The kitten tilted his head, the shrew still squirming.

I wasn't sure how to make sense of it, all this raw beauty, the uncomfortable parts left in, the dirt clods with the tasseled corn, the flowers wilting, the berries with the thorns, the adorable kitten with the half-dead shrew. All I can say is that the whole scene pulsed with God, and I could feel the reverberations down to my bones.

But now, here in the pew, God was gone. At least it felt that way to me. I found myself daydreaming through the scripture reading, but I had heard it so many times before. It was the ninth chapter of Mark in which Jesus asks his disciples what they'd been quarrelling about, and they were silent, embarrassed to admit that they'd been arguing over whom among them was the greatest disciple. Jesus turned to them and

said, "Whoever wants to be first must be last of all and servant of all."
Then he took a child and . . .

Father Joe kept reading, as I worked off my frustration on my
cuticles. Just how was I supposed to be a servant of all without anyone
to serve? I'd never been a part of a church in which all we did was
worship. Was I supposed to soak up God all over Clermont, only to
steep in it myself, or squeeze it out on just my family and friends? My
family and I had always had everything we needed, and now in France
we had too much.

Every day I'd live the fairytale scene—the old woman opening her
shutters, the wisteria climbing up the side of a stacked stone house,
the castle on the green hill in the distance—and thank God for this
beautiful dream.

How could I pay God back? Chat a little more with my neighbors?
Hold the door for a stranger at the market? That wasn't serving God;
it was just being polite.

How I missed serving. Having a calendar full of projects made me
feel that I'd earned my place at the altar table.

What else could I do for God? Put more money in the plate? I
didn't believe in buying my way in, and besides, what would the extra
money go for? Repairing the pews to make me more comfortable?

Father Joe began the homily, but all I heard were strings of words.
Everyone else was clearly entranced by Father Joe's message, leaning
forward in their pews, following his every gesture. I couldn't blame it
on distractions. They'd put the Flames of Hell away until it got cold
again, Sam didn't ask for a single visit to my human dairy barn, and
we'd found a sturdy pew this time. So why was I about to jump out of
my skin?

I tried to focus on Father Joe's words, doodling on the program. I
fumbled through my purse for a mint and played with Sam's hair, shift-
ing in my seat, trying to get comfortable.

When it was time for communion, I whispered to Todd, "I'll go
first, OK?"

See, God? I'm not afraid. Fill me with your peace.

The little girl in line in front of me started bickering with her big
sister, interrupting my prayer. Were their parents going to ignore it?

I felt for them, but they let their children argue during communion? Didn't they view it as sacred?

I'd see the same kind of thing back home. Our minister started confusing things by opening the Lord's Supper to anyone who'd find it meaningful, and all the rules about being baptized first went out the window. I liked the sentiment, but what about the sanctity of the act? Before I was baptized I wanted bread and juice too. Who wouldn't?

When it came my turn I took a tiny pinch, hearing the words of Father Joe and Madame Pink Suit, "Take, eat." I pulled a thin wad between my fingers, no bigger than the piece I'd get back home. I chewed it, surprised to find that it had a taste, so different from the floury bit of cracker with which I was accustomed.

"The cup of salvation," said Father Joe, handing me the chalice. The metal felt cold and thin on my lips. I sipped and the sweetness of the Port rolled over my tongue.

"How was it?" Ben whispered as I took my seat.

"Then why are you making that face?"

"Don't bother her, Ben," Sarah said. She patted my knee. "It's OK, Mama. Just don't think about other people's spit."

There was soft laughter from the congregation. Had they heard her? No. Father Joe's toddler had escaped from his mother in the pew and wrapped his arms around the priest's pants leg, grinning at everyone watching him. Father Joe patted his head as his son snuggled close, sucking his thumb.

"This was totally planned," Father Joe joked. "He's reenacting the Gospel reading." The Gospel reading . . . ? I must have missed that part. I scanned the program for the verses. "Then he took a little child and put it among them; and taking it in his arms he said to them, 'Whoever welcomes one such child in my name welcomes me, and whoever welcomes me welcomes not me but the one who sent me.'"

With his blond curls, Tommy looked like the boy Jesus in the stained glass window, his eyes staring through me. Whoever welcomes one such child in my name . . .

All this child talk—welcome the child, come as a child—was this what God wanted me to hear? I'd always loved the image before, but now it just got under my skin. If I had to spend my days wandering around clueless, I was an expert already and didn't recommend it. Surely God didn't mean for me to relinquish the control befitting a full grown woman, to live my new life depending on others. I liked being the one who served, who helped.

As we read the post-communion prayer, Sammy reached up to rustle my hair and trace around my ear with a finger. I kissed his cheek, imagining his hand was God's, stroking my head as I pulled on his pants leg. Whether or not I could earn my way in, I would stay close to God. Whether I could feel his presence or not, I'd hold onto faith, certain that God wouldn't turn away from me.

In my mind I would climb into that flower-festooned Peugeot, soak up the sweet smell of the flowers and the corn, seeing and feeling God in the petals and the dirt, the blackberries and the thorns, even in the kitten and the half-dead shrew. God's creation throbbed all around me, and the heartbeat was the Spirit's. As much as I wanted to drive, because I'm stubborn and like to control things, I knew I couldn't and shouldn't. Take it, God, I prayed. I'll try my best not to call out directions.

So that's how a flowered and fruited and vegetabled car earned a card in my stack of wonders and saints. The tagline?

Toss God the keys. Enjoy the ride.

And the prayer I'd ask?

God who speaks through dirt clods and corn silks, through sunflowers and dahlias, shrews and helpless children, hear us as we tug on your pants leg. Touch us with your peace. Drive for us, no matter how much we beg to grip the steering wheel.

Chapter 7
A Singer for the Man of Sorrows

"It's just a little day trip," Todd said, handing me my jacket. "Aren't you always saying that's what Saturdays are for?"

What had happened to my husband? Why wasn't he planting himself in his easy chair, protesting that after the week of work he needed to lie around and do nothing, that we'd have at least three or four years in France to see all the sights?

I knew very well what he was doing, the sneaky man. He knew that playing tourist always made me happy, and after our get-together with the neighbors the night before, let's just say my ego needed a little boost.

Before we moved to France, I had always imagined my first garden party. Edith Piaf's music would be playing, and I'd mill about the guests like a carefree Audrey Hepburn, snacking on pâté and speaking perfect French.

Reality was so much less attractive.

As I sat on the Roches' terrace sandwiched between Madame Mallet and my husband, Sam busied himself on my lap, swinging his toy in my face. My five neighbors sat on the edge of their seats, hanging on my every mutilated word. It was so kind of them to invite us and I was glad for the chance to get to know them, but I was a little stressed out. For the first time in my entire life I drank for effect. I just wished the wine would hurry up and calm me down.

Apparently I wasn't drinking fast enough. A few minutes later, Alain eyed my glass, still a third full.

"Can I pour you something else?" he asked, pointing to the cart crowded with bottles of liquor and wine.

"Oh no," I said. "It is good."

"Are you sure, my dear?" Madame Mallet asked.

"Maybe something American . . . un whisky?" asked Monsieur Mallet.

"Non, merci."

Thankfully my dear husband stepped in and moved the conversation along to Madame Fauriaux's roses. I looked out into the sunset and tried to relax. It was such a gorgeous evening. The sun was setting behind the Puy de Dôme, the great purple mountain in the distance, and the orange light fell in a mist over the dozen communal garden plots extending from Alain and Pascale's terrace, turning the view into a movie backdrop. Beyond the clinking of our glasses and the laughter of the children, there was the buzz of a far-off motorbike. A motorbike, yes, focus on that. Be Madame Pink Suit, calm and collected.

I was just starting to feel better when I looked over at the children's table and saw my seven-year-old guzzling down champagne out of a crystal flute and dancing around with the bottle, acting like Otis the Drunk from *The Andy Griffith Show*.

In a split second I'd handed Sam off to Todd and was about to go grab Ben by the ear until Todd pulled me back down to my seat, laughing. "It's not champagne, Beck. It's *Champomy*—kiddy champagne. It's just bubbly apple juice." He translated to our puzzled neighbors and they laughed. Yes, let's all have a chuckle over silly Becky.

"But I thought . . . It looks . . ." I stuttered, trying to be a good sport.

"Don't worry, Rébecca," said Madame Mallet. "We would not allow Ben to drink a whole glass of champagne. With Sarah, of course, it's a different story. How old is she? Nine?"

Todd winked at me and I took another sip.

It sure seemed to me that while I was strolling through my French life, going gaga over sunflowers and purple volcanoes, lovely France was determined to seek out every single thing that made me uncomfortable, everything I thought I'd tied up in a neat little package back in South Carolina. Not only did it seek out any gift-wrapped awkwardness, it opened it up, took it out, and wallpapered my life with it!

Idleness made me uneasy, and now I had nothing to do. Nakedness embarrassed me, and now naked breasts were everywhere. I hated looking foolish, and now I was the village idiot. I was trying my best to let God drive the car, but maybe we could take the front seat for a bit.

Todd was right. A side trip to the little village of Ambert might be a nice diversion. Not only did Ambert have a Musée de Papier, where the kids could watch paper being made the old-fashioned way, with screens and presses and flower petals worked right in, but its Fourme d'Ambert cheese was known throughout France. We might be able to tour the museum of steam engines too, if we could ever get through lunch.

How long does it take to make a few crêpes?

I stood out in the sunshine, taking the second shift of Sam duty, trying to stay warm in the sudden late September chill. I didn't mind too much. French restaurants were no place to take a toddler. Even the most casual places proved hazardous, with their checkered tablecloths brushing Sam's feet, tempting him to give them a good yank. The mere sight of wine and water goblets transformed Sam into a baby octopus, obsessed with getting a glass in each hand, apparently so he could toast himself.

When we first arrived in France and went running off into the countryside on Saturdays, we'd forgo the humiliation and stop by a boulangerie for sandwiches or take a picnic and eat by the side of the road. But eventually we longed for a hot meal off a real plate. After a couple of lunchtime fiascos we'd finally discovered the key to happiness: Todd and I would take turns entertaining Sam outside until the lunch was served, when we'd bring him to the table along with the meal, as if he were a condiment. This seemed to please the other diners and wait staff as well.

So there I stood, watching Sam bending over to finger a snail on the cobblestone street. It was a quaint little alley, so narrow and pictur-esque. We'd walked up to the restaurant just as the shopkeepers were locking their doors and disappearing upstairs for lunch. Now it was quiet, with only Sam's little murmurings, the scratch of my shoes on the cobblestones, and the creak of someone opening a window upstairs to set a pot on the ledge to cool.

When was lunch? The sooner we ate, the sooner we could move on with the day and enjoy what Ambert had to show us. Then we could go home and I could start looking for that path God had for me, for the lessons he wanted me to learn along the way.

What was taking so long? Maybe we should go in and check.

Stop. Look.

Yes, maybe I was being impatient. Release control, remember? Checking on lunch wouldn't make it come any faster. It's good to take time to notice things, I thought, as I looked around. There was a doorknocker shaped like a lady's hand, a pretty display in the gift shop window, the sound of my stomach growling. Sam's little fingers were just closing in on the snail shell when a loud noise startled me.

A man in tattered clothes was bounding up the cobblestone street in my direction, three German shepherds following at his heels as he burst out singing like a human bell, "bloum, bloy, maw, baum." What in the world?

He was big and we were completely alone.

I looked to the window of the *crêperie*, hoping to see Todd's face behind the lace curtain, but the lady had seated us by the fireplace. Todd wouldn't be able to see me from there.

He was getting closer, blouming and bloying as the dogs jumped along. Don't flinch, I told myself. I scooped Sam on my hip and straightened up, hoping to appear taller, more confident. "It's OK, buddy," I whispered, wanting to comfort us both against the scary dogs and the pony-tailed man with a walking stick. Sam didn't care. He was showing me the snail shell pinched between his fingers. The dogs jumped, as if trying to catch invisible Frisbees.

They were just ten yards away. Sam saw them and dropped the shell.

"Do you see that lamp there?" I said to Sam in my calmest voice, nodding to the gift shop window. "The one with the boat on it?"

"Did you say 'boat'?" the big man said in a British accent.

Thank heavens. He wasn't scary after all—in spite of his layers of shirts, camouflage pants frayed at the hem, toes sticking out of sandals, blue from the cold. He wasn't about to start yelling at me or asking me for money. I bet he was a student—no, too many wrinkles for that— maybe a professor then, an eccentric. I nodded at him and he nodded back, tapped his walking stick twice on the road, and then trotted over to me, as if I was an old friend.

"You're not French!" he said, pulling his dogs down from sniffing at me. "What in God's name are you doing here?"

I explained and loosened my grip on Sam.

"Ah, an American: I hear it in your voice," he said. "Well, I'm a Brit myself, and I'm thinking of buying one of these buildings." He poked the *drogerie* storefront with his stick. He cupped his hand to stare in at the teapots displayed neatly on glass shelves, and then turned abruptly to face me. "Do you know Bill Gates?"

Was he joking? "Well," I said, "not personally."

"I'm like him." Poking at the cobblestones, he added, "except without all his money."

One of the dogs licked at Sam's shoes, and Sam began to whimper.

The man zoomed nose to nose with Sam, startling me, and took on a singsong voice. "Oh don't be afraid of my sweethearts!" he sang, grabbing one of the dogs and rubbing its belly. "We're only babies—just like you." He kissed the dog right on the mouth and then turned to me, suddenly serious. "You're an American, see, the greatest producer of arms in the world—then Russia, yes, and France, and we too in Britain."

OK, so I was in for a lecture.

"Ever see a child with one leg and the white bone showing?"

I shook my head. This guy was crazy. Where was Todd?

"That's a land mine," he said. "I was trained as a doctor, you see." He paused a moment, glared hard at the ground, and then faced me again, his voice becoming gravely, as if he were about to cry. "I'm a Christian, you know, and so I sing. For God's sake, does that make sense?"

"Um," I responded, "well . . ."

All at once his blue eyes reddened and filled with tears. "You see," he said, his voice breaking, "I have to find a way to make it better. . . . for the small ones—like this one here." He puffed up his cheeks at Sam like a blowfish, tears falling from his eyes. "So I sing. I don't know if it makes sense, but that is what I do." He paused for a moment, and then nodded decidedly. "That is what I must do. This world is so big," he said, his tears leaving a jagged path down his chapped face, "I must do it."

This full grown man was crying like a child. It was hard to keep from looking away, but I didn't want to abandon him, to show him in effect that his honesty embarrassed me. He didn't try to control his emotions the least little bit, but offered his tears on a platter for me, his inner self exposed.

I looked into his bloodshot eyes. I'd spent so much energy tucking in my feelings and fears, trying to look like I knew what I'm doing. And yet here he was, a stranger weeping not for himself, but for the misery in the world. Who did that, walking the streets, crying and singing for mankind? What could I say? I opened my mouth to come up with something, and he spun on his heels and took a giant step up the hill.

"Cheerio," he shouted back to me, and bounded up the street. His dogs trotted behind him, and he gave a loud sniffle and started to sing again. "rye, bloum, maw, grow, oh, woe." The dogs began jumping along, resuming their dance.

I watched him follow the winding path around the corner, wondering what had just happened. Had he really said those things? That he sings for God's sake, to make the world better? Was our interaction just an accidental run-in with a random schizophrenic, maybe a Christian man who used to have his act together but lost his marbles along the way? Or should I see it as some kind of message for me, a side stop on the new path God had for me? If so, did the entire journey have to be this weird?

But it was beautiful, too, in an odd way. I knew I was supposed to let go of my need to control, but surely God didn't intend on me running around town with my psyche hanging out, singing in the streets.

Still, the man's honesty spoke to me. This kind of nakedness I admired, at least to a point. Immediately I put him climbing up a cobblestone street on a holy card in my mind, Saint Singer with his walking stick and his blue toes, the dogs at his heels.

The tagline was easy:

Sing for God's sake.

The prayer came easily, too.

> Dear God, who sees beneath our window dressing, who knows the dark and light corners of our hearts that we hide from others, make us brave enough to risk being our authentic selves as we make our way through life. Forgive the time we spend trying to impress others and the energy we spend hiding our insecurities. Give us the courage of the singer to share our tears when they come. Help us do what we can to make life better in the world, even if we're afraid that it won't make sense to others. It will make sense to you. Remind us that this is enough, Lord, and that we are enough.

As I pushed Sam up to the table, moving the glasses out of his reach, Sarah asked, "Who was that crazy guy who was talking to you? We could hear him all the way in here."

"I don't know," I answered. "He said he was singing for God."

"I couldn't understand a word he was singing," said Ben.

"Well, maybe it's because you're not God," Sarah said, as she laughed and asked for more water.

Chapter 8
Fairy Godmother Moves In

If I could write prayers for my growing deck of saints and wonders, surely by now I could pray a simple prayer in the shade of our cherry tree!

Five minutes after I'd parked myself on its roots, I fell into daydreams. My eleven-month-old sat beside me, eating grass.

"No, Sammy," I said, brushing it out of his chubby hands. I'd spread out the blanket with a couple of toys, hoping that Sam could play and I could pray and meditate. Our garden could be my private sanctuary, our tall hedges the stone walls, the open sky my cathedral ceiling. Maybe if I let my thoughts wander, they'd take me to God.

Nope, I thought, leaning over to flick off a blade of grass stuck to Sammy's cheek. My thoughts hadn't taken me to God; they'd brought me to how pretty the tree was and how nice my neighbor's trumpet sounded. Pretty soon I was considering starting piano lessons again or learning to watercolor or maybe even copy van Goghs on big canvases as Jessie did. And as I had been daydreaming ways to amuse myself, my son had turned into a ruminating calf.

I had tried changing my biblical scenery and flipped over to Proverbs, where I ran into the Wife of Noble Character (chapter 31), the woman I was supposed to be, I guess. But as I forced my eyes to read the verses, I kept feeling sorry for her. She must be so tired, this noble wife, with all that getting up before dawn, cooking and sewing and planting and selling. "She does not eat the bread of idleness," said verse 27.

Try coming to France, lady. Just try it.

I was enjoying my new life, but maybe I needed some accountability, someone standing over my shoulder, whispering in my ear whenever I got off track, making sure I was making use of my time: "What do you want, a fairy godmother?"

I laughed to myself, shook off the blanket, and led Sam back to the garage to finish the laundry.

Two days later Cindy and I abandoned all chores to stand dumbstruck in a used furniture store, face to face with an eight-foot-tall fairy godmother. Was God granting my wish? She was the most gorgeous thing I'd ever seen.

The tag labeled it a *comtoise*, the French version of a grandfather clock—or should I say a grandmother clock. With her round hips and mottled red paint, she might have danced off the stage of *Beauty and the Beast*. Her face was framed by two silver horns of flowers and berries cascading down to her shoulders, and within her chest hung a brass pendulum painted with more flowers and ribbons. On her skirt was an old painting, almost rubbed off from years of dusting and cleaning. I could barely make out a country scene, with an old man smoking a pipe, two horses and a boy—a puzzle of sorts to figure out. She'd be so perfect in my house, counting the minutes, ticking off the message I needed to hear:

Time's a gift, so stop your daydreaming. Wake up and get busy. Do something. Take a lesson from the singing man. Get on your feet and find a way to make the world better.

Just yesterday at coffee, Jessie had preached her own sermon. "Let me give you some advice," she said. "It's impossible to live in such a beautiful place and not want to have a little beauty of your own. Start looking now. Buy an armoire or a table to take home with you. I'm telling you, if you try to resist, it'll just take over your brain anyway. It's better just to go ahead and give in."

I laughed. She was joking, wasn't she? But it did make sense, at least the part about taking over my brain. It was startling to be suddenly dropped into such an enormous vat of beauty and left to bob around in it as it worked on me, seeping into my pores. I hadn't even realized how much it was missing from my life until this move.

I could see her point, that if I didn't bring beauty in, it would force itself in, into my thoughts and dreams. It already had! It wasn't the laundry piles or our little yellow house in South Carolina that was clouding my brain, making any of my old determination and ambition to get things done wilt like petals in the sun. It was the sunflower fields, the rippling tile roofs, the loveliness of Madame Pink Suit kissing her son goodbye.

By the time I'd washed the morning breakfast dishes, I'd decided that maybe Jessie's advice made sense. Beauty was everywhere, whispering to me constantly, drowning out my own prayers. Even the crazy man had his own beauty, a slightly dangerous, primitive kind: the paleness of his eyes, as if he'd cried all the color out, his long hair pulled back, his ragtag clothes.

And now here she was, this fairy godmother in red, waiting for me, clicking off the minutes, ready to chime the hours of my soon-to-find productivity.

"Too bad the glass is broken," Cindy said. I hadn't even noticed the shards stacked on the floor, as if someone might actually glue them back together. No problem. Todd did stained glass as a hobby. It'd be an easy repair.

"So what's the damage?" Cindy asked as I reached for the tag hanging from the tiny latch on the pendulum cabinet.

"It just says it was made in 1903." I flipped it over: 4,200 francs. My heart sank.

"You know, that sounds like a lot of money," Cindy said, "but what is that—$700? It'd cost at least ten times that much back home."

I mopped my kitchen floor that afternoon, hoping to scrub the clock out of my mind. It didn't work. Three days later I packed the diaper bag for the store again. Surely someone would have bought it by now. I'd look around, it'd be gone, and I could stop wasting my time pining away.

I had just put Sam in the car seat when Monsieur Pollet, our Gene Kelly lookalike postman, buzzed up on his motorbike with a package for me. My heart skipped a beat, as if I'd been caught. He dismounted his bike, shook my hand as usual, nodded at my door, and said, "*Après vous* (after you), *madame*." Was it considered uncivilized to sign for it outside? I pulled Sam out of his car seat, led the postman into our entryway, and felt a shiver as he shut the door behind us.

As he handed me the slip, I scolded myself: He's not trying to rob you or seduce you. Just because you're being sneaky doesn't mean everyone else is.

After he drove off I opened the box. It was a care package from my friend Christine back in South Carolina: a package of Oreos, a Greenville newspaper, and a *Southern Living* magazine. "We talked about you on Sunday," she wrote in an enclosed note, "By now you've probably gotten all French on us, eating croissants and snails and dancing to accordion music. We want you to come back some day. Don't get too swept away!"

It was too late.

The clock cost $700. We only spend that kind of money on things we absolutely need, like a new heat pump or a couch that we'd sit on every day until it wore out.

Sam fussed in the stroller, so I took a loop around the store to let him fall asleep, carefully avoiding the aisle with the clock. Wouldn't buying a clock like that be awfully extravagant? Wouldn't it be wasteful? Don't I have clocks all over the house and a watch right here on my wrist?

But it wasn't about telling the time. It was about telling that time is a beautiful gift, acknowledging it as a treasure to be used well; to be celebrated; to be honored with flowers and tendrils and an old man and a horse; to let it dance in my house, where my children could hear it and see it, watching time pass with the gentle rocking of a lullaby.

What more perfect souvenir would I find of our time here?

It didn't matter anyway. They'd probably sold it.

They hadn't.

It was right where we'd left it, a lady with a powdered white face and fine Roman numeral features, standing tall among all those armoires and buffets, dining sets and headboards. I pulled up a chair and sat down to admire it—or her. She was all ablush, waiting for me.

The store owner, a big man in les bleus and a white lab coat, came over and introduced himself. "How wonderful that you're American," he said, shaking my hand. "I've noticed you like the clock. She's beautiful, yes?"

I nodded, afraid to speak again and sound like a fool.

"And she works," he said, and with his stubby fingers he showed me how to slide the tiny hook from the latch and open up her chest. He gently removed the long pendulum and handed it to me. It was lighter than I expected, made of thin brass, embossed with flowers and painted with iridescent pastels. Behind the pendulum dangled two pieces of ordinary twine.

"You attach the weights here," he directed, and picked the thick cylinders off the floor and tied them on. "And then you wind her up."

As he wound the key in her face, the gears ticked off and the weights slowly rose in the lower cabinet. He replaced the pendulum, turned the hands on her face to the correct time, gave a little flick to get the pendulum, and off she went. The pendulum clicked in rhythm as it moved side to side.

"As you can see, Madame Ramsey, she keeps excellent time and is ready to go to your home, that is, except for the work with the glass. But I know many shops that would fix that for you."

As he began listing them off, I wondered what Todd would think.

Monsieur Rousseaux followed me to the door when we were ready to leave. "She attracts a lot of attention," he said. "Many people have been admiring her."

"I need to talk with my husband," I said.

Monsieur Rousseau was clearly going for the hard sell. He didn't know that I was sold already. We'd bring the clock home and I'd put her in the hub of our home, next to the dining table, where we could see her from the living room. There she could remind us, but with a soft touch: Time's a-wasting, my dear. Make use of this beautiful life you've been given.

Now I just had to convince Todd.

That evening I confessed. "It was like love at first sight," I said, and gave him a whole presentation on why we should buy the clock, what a perfect souvenir it would be—reminding us of both the beauty of France and the treasure of time. Then I tried to appeal to his practical side. I dragged him over to the computer and showed him the pictures I'd found on the internet of similar clocks.

"See what a good investment it'd be?" I said, pointing to the listed price. "That's thirteen times as much."

"It's only an investment if you plan to sell it, Beck. But it is nice. And I like the idea of bringing back a beautiful clock. It's a great way to remind us of the luxury of time we have here—you know . . . eat, drink, and be merry! I love it. Let's go see it next weekend."

"Eat, drink, and be merry?"

"Yeah, you know . . . your new philosophy here in France."

"What new philosophy? I don't have a new philosophy."

"I'm not saying it's a bad philosophy, honey." Todd said. "It's a Bible verse, for goodness sake. You know . . . that one from Ecclesiastes. I've always loved that verse. How does it go again? Something like, 'Seize the day. Eat your bread and drink your wine with joy . . . God takes pleasure in your pleasure.' Let's go see the clock next weekend. I'd love to see it."

Eat, drink, and be merry? Where did that come from?

Apparently Ecclesiastes 9:7. I looked it up that night. According to Todd, it was my new motto, a long way from Miss Proverbs, with her purple robe and dishpan hands. But he was right, I guess. I had found a happiness here that I'd never experienced before. Could I really embrace both scriptures? I decided to let Proverbs Wife and Ecclesiastes Old Man fight it out while I went to bed.

Saturday morning I stood in the store aisle beside the clock, presenting her to Todd and the kids as if she were a new member of the family. "You're right," Todd said. "It's gorgeous."

Todd wiped a finger on the side of the cabinet face. "Are those worm holes?"

Worm holes?

"See the little holes right here?" he said, looking closer. I hadn't even noticed them. "That's where they've burrowed in and eaten out the wood. But I don't see any dust, so it's probably been treated." He examined the sides. "The paint is so uneven," he said. "Look, here it's really thick, and here it looks like somebody wiped most of it off."

"I like that about it," I said. "It's . . . chic."

Todd laughed and bent down to examine the feet, one a plain Jane square and the other curved like a lady's shoe. "They probably replaced it after one too many knocks with a broom or mop," I explained.

Monsieur Rousseaux opened the latch to the clock's inner workings and stepped out of the way. One look at the gear box and my engineer husband was smitten.

"It's not just a clock," Todd said to Ben and Sarah. "It's a piece of art."

Ben looked askew at his dad. "You're talking like a preacher. Can we go now?"

Todd did look converted. He started taking measurements to replace the glass, and started thinking out loud about how he would bolt the clock to the wall. He didn't want our new piece of art toppling over on one of the children. "You know how Sam pulls up on everything now. With those heavy workings and weights, she'd flatten him in a second."

How I love that man.

Two days later a guy in navy leggings and a gray sweatshirt brought the clock into my living room. "Here, madame," he said, handing me the shards of glass. "You're going to need some glue."

When I brought the children home from school they flocked to her side, as if she were our family's own personal fairy godmother. Todd came home from work and bolted her to the wall and wound her up, sending the flowery pendulum swinging side to side, back and forth.

As I looked at her, I realized I'd been wrong. The pendulum wasn't at all like a wagging finger. No, it was more like the priest's swinging incense, calling me back to my dream, back to the cathedral, back to the bread and wine. Would the clock quiet my soul, my mind? We would see.

We wound up her chimes, and she got so excited that she rang out every fifteen minutes, high and tinny, as if she was tickled to be home. The kids laughed. "Do it again! Do it again!" they begged. After a few choruses of laughter, they dragged their backpacks to the seats at our table closest to her, opened up their homework, and let her watch, ticking off the minutes until dinnertime.

That night I stayed up late, straightening the house, doing the last bit of laundry. Todd went on to bed, but I had a few more things to do. Once my load of whites was folded and sorted, I put my basket down by the clock to admire her again.

Now that I had something so beautiful of my own to enjoy whenever I wanted, I bet my thoughts might be less likely to wander. The pendulum swayed back and forth, back and forth, beckoning me, hypnotizing me, encouraging me, with every tick to what . . . slow down? Cherish the loveliness around me?

Wait. That's not right. Wasn't I supposed to be productive . . . to do . . . to find ways to make life better?

What about my fairy godmother? An inner voice spoke up: A fairy godmother gets you ready for the ball—she doesn't dole out to-do lists. You've got her mixed up with the evil stepmother!

Hmm. Maybe I'd leave it to her to referee between the Proverbs 31 lady and the old man of Ecclesiastes who was ready to party.

I crawled into bed beside my sleeping husband and laid still in the lamplight, listening to the quiet of the house, to the sound of my cat hopping onto our bedroom chair, the clock ticking like a metronome, keeping time with Todd's breathing. My daily meditation, I thought, glancing at the book on my bedside table. Maybe not tonight. I fluffed my pillow, pulled the quilt over myself, and wiggled my toes to the rhythm.

A tiny alarm went off in my head: But you always read a meditation!

What was this? I'd bought the clock to guard me from distractions, and now I had an eight-foot-tall distraction ticking loudly in my living room, singing, "$700, $700. You just blew $700."

Stop it. Go to sleep.

I turned off the light and focused on the rhythm, matching my breathing to Todd's.

Calm down.

Rest easy.

Balance takes

A lot of time.

I would find balance. God would help me.

Two weeks later I was still searching for it, but at least our clock had made herself at home. She'd watch over the kids while they slurped their cereal or practiced their spelling, while I braided Sarah's hair or chased after Sam. She clicked off moments while we laughed ourselves silly or bickered and slammed doors.

She deserved a saint card of her own. She watched over us when we seized the day and ate our bread and wine with joy and when we didn't. She was my Proverbs 31 wife, ticking off time around the clock, marking it as we slept, when we worked hard and when we ate the bread of idleness, enraptured by the beauty around us.

The card would be easy. There would be a portrait of herself on the front, with her rosy crown and round hips, her mismatched shoes and powdered face. Her flowery pendulum would be in mid swing.

Swirly letters would dance out the tagline:

Seize the day.

(Sorry, Proverbs lady, but it seems to fit.) And of course there I would have to add "bibbidi-bobbidi-boo" to the card somewhere. I owed it to my fairy godmother.

And the prayer?

Dear Father-Mother of all time, help us find balance as we tick off the moments of our lives. Wind within our hearts an inner rhythm that follows yours. Whisper in our ears when we get off track, when balance goes askew, and reset us to your time. Remind us gently or with brassy chimes, if we need it, that every minute we have is a gift from you. Amen.

Chapter 9
Jessie and the Merry Women

At ten o'clock on Sunday morning Jessie and Cindy and I stood at a crosswalk in the shadow of Église St. Thomas, bracing ourselves against the wind that was nudging us back toward the church. As soon as the light changed, we'd cross the street to the Sunday morning flea market. The bells chimed the hour, calling the parish, "Come to church, come to church."

Some of the faithful were answering the call. Three little old ladies wearing dresses and heels waited at the opposite corner.

It's like a scene out of *West Side Story*, I laughed to myself, trying to shake off my guilt. The Sharks and the Jets—the French church ladies versus the American moneychangers. The joke didn't make me feel any better. If I were back in South Carolina, I'd be teaching Sunday School this morning, not shopping. Why did I need to go shopping anyway? I just bought an eight-foot-tall clock. What more did I need?

The light turned green, and as we passed the women I fought the urge to reach out and clasp their hands and say, "I'm a church lady too!"

They looked a bit afraid of us. Jessie had probably scared them, talking too loudly in English, wearing her army boots and cut-off shorts again in spite of the late September chill.

I offered the women a meek smile. One returned a grim nod, then looked down at my feet and furrowed her brow. Was it my clogs that puzzled her, or did she think that I should have on a skirt and turn right back to worship?

Yet there I was. When Cindy called, Todd told her that of course I'd want to go, that he'd watch the kids, no problem. He thought he was helping, sure that I needed a break from being mommy, to get out on my own with friends with no baby hands grabbing at me. But did I really need to go?

"Oh stop," my fairy grandmother clucked at me as I slipped on my shoes, wagging her pendulum. "Enjoy yourself. Seize the day!"

Now that we were within sight of the flea market, really the asphalt parking lot of the Champion grocery store, I wondered if Madame Mallet was right. She'd given me her opinion of Les Puces des Salins as I waited outside for Cindy.

"The flea market?" she asked. "Rébecca, if you're going shopping, why don't you go to some reputable place, where the merchandise isn't stolen or full of termites?" I shrugged my shoulders and she added, "Be careful. Les Puces des Salins is swarming with pickpockets."

Jessie said that Madame Mallet was nuts; that the market was perfectly safe, but I'd already determined that Jessie had her own brand of craziness. When we picked her up this morning she had insisted we come in to see the new painting she was finishing, a copy of *The Birth of Venus*.

"Henri just left with the girls for a walk in the vineyard. We usually linger over a nice slow breakfast on days like this, but these breasts are driving me crazy," she said, nodding at Venus. "I wanted to get the right roundness, you know, without giving her a boob job."

This struck me as hilarious, but I wasn't sure whether to laugh or not. It was hard to know how to act in Jessie's house, surrounded by huge paintings at every turn, bright, swirling van Goghs and big canvases of nudes. I'd never seen a house decorated quite like hers, in happy quirkiness, with bright yellow walls, a mix of Spanish furniture and mid-century American.

As we got back into Cindy's car, I looked back at her house nestled against the vineyard, its red tiled roof rippling into the hills behind it. "You've got a vineyard in your backyard? How lucky!"

"It is paradise, isn't it?" said Jessie. "I just love walking through the vineyard on lazy mornings like this. Every once in a while I'll miss spending my Sunday mornings in bed with the *New York Times*, but then I look out my window and that all fades away."

She used to spend her lazy Sunday mornings in bed with the paper? The only times I'd ever done that was when my whole family went to Ocean Isle on vacation. Sunday mornings at our house were anything but leisurely. It was the only time the children wore ironed clothes and

I put on heels. Just getting three kids ready for Sunday School and out of the house was enough for me and Todd to work up a sweat. It was work, but it was worth it. Most of the time, I really enjoyed it. And the rest of the time . . . ? I was trying to do the right thing.

As we crossed the street and walked closer to the vendors, the scent of coffee drifted over from the coffee truck. There were a dozen men standing at tall bistro tables pulled out onto the asphalt. Did they notice the bells? Did they not feel called to the pews?

We crossed the park and I slung my purse across my body, just in case Madame Mallet was right about pickpockets. "Ladies," Jessie announced loudly, "I present to you, heaven!" Cindy giggled. I smiled but kept my eye on the homeless man picking through a trash can five yards away. "The table is set before us. Let us feast!"

Feast? I wasn't sure. Jessie kept grabbing my arm before I could even see much, gushing, "See? Didn't I tell you? Isn't this great? It's the real France. You just don't know people until you see their junk. And their junk is gorgeous!"

Then I noticed a man in a gray sweater and jeans unloading a tall armoire from his truck and a little side table with the cutest curvy legs. My heart quickened. We'd definitely have our own church service tonight, I thought, smoothing down my guilt like a Sunday morning cowlick, so my soul was free to take it all in.

Some stands were neatly organized, with neat stacks of books, plastic-wrapped linens, rickety old chairs lined up in rows. Other tables were heaped with piles of things, ripped drapes mixed in with old clothes and kitchenware. And some folks just had rows of cardboard boxes where people knelt, thumbing through the contents—clocks and books and clothes and dishes.

"Look, Beck, there's sure to be saint cards!" Jessie said, thumbing through a metal tin of yellowed postcards. I joined in, flipping through a cigar box beside her, but I couldn't help but examine the rest of the treasures on the table. There was a statue of a woman in a brown robe and headscarf, her right arm broken off, a leatherbound prayer book, and beside it a plastic lawn gnome that looked like one of the seven dwarfs.

"Look y'all," I said, patting its head, "It's Sneezy."

Cindy glanced over at it and her eyes widened. "More like Sleazy," she said. "Look again." The gnome was pornographic. Its pants were unzipped with its anatomy out on display. Jessie found this hysterical.

The flea market was grimy and dusty and full of broken-down things. Jessie walked ahead, striding from table to table in search of saints. "Not just cards," she said, as we tried to keep up. "Last week I saw a great—" She stopped short and grinned. "No, I'm going to surprise you. I'm going to buy it if it's still here. You won't believe how great it is! You'll see. I'll be back."

As Cindy and I walked the aisles, stopping to examine plates and embroidered linens, hats and toys and paintings, some splattered with mud or torn, others in gilt frames, the aroma of coffee blended with the smell of dog pee and of sausages sizzling in the café trucks. I could also pick out the scent of furniture polish and mildew and the slightest hint of body odor.

The market had everything you could think of. There were tall, perfect armoires and buffets carved with flowers or dead birds hanging upside down beside sets of chairs with various missing parts. There were boxes of mugs and crystal, chandeliers in pieces, old lawn furniture, and stacks of old magazines. As I flipped through a 1917 issue of *Illustration,* a silverfish scurried across the page.

"It's still here! I found it!" Jessie shouted, startling me. "You gotta come see!" She dragged Cindy and me across two aisles, to a three-foot-high statue of Joan of Arc. "Isn't she great?" Jessie asked.

Was she serious? She looked like a mannequin straight out of a window at Prix Unique, with her frozen pensive stare and her stiff pageboy hairstyle. Her face had an odd suntan, and she held her flag and looked bravely into the distance, an armored leg stepping forth from the plaster folds of her blue tunic. Jessie was going to buy that and put it in her house?

"Where do you think it came from?" Cindy asked.

"I'm sure it's out of a church," she said, gazing at the statue. "So many are closing their doors here. She could have been stolen—I don't know. That'd be a trick, as big as she is. Don't you think she's beautiful?"

"She really is," Cindy said, looking her over.

"What do you think, Becky?"

"I think it's great," I said. If she really liked it, I wanted to be encouraging, and Joan did have a certain charm. I preferred the girlish Joan in my wallet, and I couldn't see putting something like that in my house, but in Jessie's home? I could see it.

Jessie told the man she wanted to *réfléchir* (reflect) a little about Joan, and we walked on. "Forget the saint cards, Becky," Jessie said. "Why not buy yourself a saint? There's a Saint Anne at a table at the end that has the prettiest face, and she's just 150 francs . . . What's that—twenty-five dollars? Can you believe that? Religious iconography is the best thing in France. I'm starting a collection myself."

I wasn't so sure. Besides, there were all sorts of things I found beautiful—prayer books worn from use, crosses of all kinds, crude and ornate, hand carved and upholstered in velvet, the nap rubbed off from being stroked and held for so many years.

As Jessie stopped to pick through a cardboard box, something special caught my eye. Propped behind a box of old photographs was someone's framed baptismal certificate, colorized like an antique postcard in blue and aqua and pink. The gold border of grapevines and filigree matched the flaky gilt frame and divided the certificate into eight little scenes, some with a gentle pink-lipped Jesus, others with Mary and some saints I didn't recognize, and three at the bottom showing boys and girls in the sacraments of baptism, first communion, and confirmation. At the bottom, filled out in big, loopy fountain-penned handwriting, was the name René Ducout. It listed the baptismal date as August 3, 1909, and his first communion as May 30, 1920. At the top was the title, " *Précieux Souvenir Si Vous* Êtes *Fidèle*" (Precious Souvenir If You Are Faithful). Was René Ducout faithful? And if so, what was his precious souvenir doing on the table at Les Puces des Salins?

I looked around to show my friends, but they were gone. There was Cindy, farther down the aisle, but Jessie had disappeared.

"You like it?" The scruffy-faced vendor with a face like a weasel bounced a cigarette in his lips.

I felt a sudden twinge of fear and clutched my purse against me. I nodded my answer, not wanting to reveal my foreign status.

He started talking and quickly lost me.

"I'm sorry," I interrupted. "My French isn't very good."

He smiled, looking me over. "Ah, you're a foreigner," he said, picking up the certificate and wiping it with the edge of his jacket. His fingernails were dirty. "You're British?"

"No, I'm American."

He elbowed the man beside him. "We have an American here." He bowed. "American Girl," he said and grinned.

I didn't know what to do. He snuffed out his cigarette in an ashtray, and I muttered *merci* and turned around, bumping right into Jessie.

"Find anything?" she asked.

I nodded and pointed to the certificate on the table. The weasel man's eyes scanned her, head to toe.

"Ah," she said, examining it. "*C'est beau!* (That's beautiful!)"

"Bonjour, madame," the man said, smiling and showing his bad teeth. "It's a fine certificate, isn't it?"

"Yes, it is," she said. "How old is it?"

The man started talking fast again. Jessie listened attentively and put it back on the table. "It's lovely; it certainly is. Thank you for telling me about it. Au revoir, monsieur."

As we walked away, Jessie whispered, "You should have rescued that."

"Rescued it?"

"Yeah, you know, buy it. Save it from getting thrown out."

"You think he'd throw it out?"

"Sure, if he doesn't sell it after a few weeks. I'm telling you, this place is teeming with sacred stuff like that. People just don't value it anymore and I can't see why. Statues and altar cloths and prayer chairs and leatherbound prayer books with the most beautiful illustrations you've ever seen, just tossed on the asphalt, like they're nothing. I don't know about you, but I'm going to save as much of it as I can."

"I love that," I said. "It's like you're God's caped crusader, saving God's stuff from danger."

Jessie laughed. "I'm not doing it for God, silly. I'm doing it for me! I do it because I love these old forgotten sacred things. You wouldn't believe what ends up at the *déchetterie.*"

"What's a déchetterie?"

"The dump . . . You know, a place where they take all the sh-. . . I mean the crap—the stuff—they don't want." Jessie laughed. "Sorry. I'm trying to work on my profanity before my girls start picking it up. But it's such a great word, déchetterie. . . . See? They de-stuff themselves—they de-"chett" themselves. The déchetterie . . . It's a great word."

I laughed. Jessie was such a puzzle.

We caught up to Cindy and spent the next hour weaving back and forth across the aisles as Jessie flitted around, talking to vendors and bargaining over books and old magazines. Wasn't she asking for trouble, chatting with everyone, people she didn't even know? The women at coffee were clear that people get the wrong idea if you talk to strangers. Still, it seemed like they all enjoyed it—Jessie, maybe, most of all. At one point she disappeared and we spent fifteen minutes searching for her.

"There you are!" Jessie said to us, as if we were the ones who'd wandered off. Cindy showed her the tray she'd bought, and Jessie reached in her bag and pulled out a leatherbound book. "Oh, I almost forgot," she said to me, putting the book back in her bag, "Guess what? I went back and bought her!"

"You bought who?" Cindy said. "What?"

"Joan! Jeanne d'Arc! Come on. I need you guys to carry my stuff."

Three minutes later Cindy and I walked down the aisle behind Jessie, carrying her purse and shopping bag as Jessie trudged past the last set of tables, hugging Joan to her side like a Siamese twin, cheek to plaster cheek. Jessie was going on about seizing the day (was my house bugged?) and how Joan was a perfect role model for her girls and how she was a beautiful piece of art. Even if the statue of Joan hadn't been as cool as it was, she said, she always wanted her girls to know that the world is an unbelievable place and unbelievable things happen, just like they happened to Joan.

The crowds parted for Jessie and Joan, men and women and children, all staring at the saint and the strange foreign lady with the cut-offs and army boots. Jessie lived what she talked. I had to give her that.

"Look at you, Becky," Cindy said. "Jessie, look, she's turning beet red!"

"Don't worry, Beck," Jessie said. "They're only staring at us because we look so fine."

This struck us so funny that we burst out in laughter. Egged on, Jessie stopped a moment to brush away a leaf that had fallen on Saint Joan's head. I bit my lip to stifle my giggles, not wanting passersby to think I was making light of their saint, but it bubbled out in fits and snorts, only making it worse.

"Don't hold it in, Beck," Jessie said. "Poor Warrior Joan—she could use a good laugh. She's been working so hard. Look at her, she's wracked with tension. That can't be good for her soul. As her official American handmaidens, the least we can do is to take her on a joy ride. You know, let the wind blow through her hair!"

It was at that moment that I knew I had a new saint for my collection, not Joan—she was already part of the deck—but Jessie, my dear, funny friend; God's caped crusader in flannel and combat boots, who flitted from stranger to stranger, drawing them into conversation, asking questions and making them laugh, and treating everyone with dignity. I needed a saint who saw beauty in things of God and God in things of beauty, no matter if she was a little unconventional. And I needed a saint who made me laugh, especially at myself.

As she opened the backseat door, wiggled Joan in beside me, and buckled her in, as if she were a child, I knew what I'd draw on the card. Jessie would be just as she was that day, cheek to cheek with Joan, striding through the aisles of Les Puces des Salins, looking like a pixie with a twinkle in her eyes and her short red hair and one white athletic sock just peeking out over the top of her left combat boot.

At the bottom the tagline would read:

Saving the sacred,
one parking lot at a time.

And the prayer?

Dear God, our rescuer, who longs to pick us out of the dirt and draw us into conversation, even as damaged as we are, thank you for seeing beauty in us, the beauty we have because we come from you. Help us to see each other as you see us, with love and dignity, even with all our brokenness on display.

Cindy started up the car, and somehow I was still praying this prayer of thankfulness. I might not be able to concentrate enough to pray in church or at will, but at that moment in the backseat with Joan it came easily. Jessie rolled down her window, and we cruised down Boulevard Jean Jaures, a Peugeot full of laughing American women and Saint Joan of Arc of France, her pageboy hairstyle unmussed by the wind.

Chapter 10
The Saint in Thigh-High Boots

Joan of Arc might get to hang out on the dining room table in Jessie's house, but my poor Joan was still in my wallet and in my brain, to be admired in private with all the other imaginary saint cards I'd dreamed up—Madame Pink Suit, the clock, the crying man, and now Jessie. Every time I sent a letter at la poste or paid for my petit crème at the café, I'd see Joan in her armor, clutching her pennant, ready to risk her life to answer God's call.

It grew to be a bit irritating.

God seemed intent on pleasing me, so why couldn't I find a way to please God? I was certainly no Joan of Arc—just yesterday's church lady turned today's hedonist, lavished with blessings and feeling a bit uncomfortable.

Autumn had arrived, bringing with it a delicious chill in the air and the smells of wood smoke and mulled wine.

I'd tried my best to find ways to be useful, taking a few newcomers on guided tours of the grocery store as Cindy had done for me, and trying to be gracious to Madame Mallet when she brought me a bag of at least 3,000 hazelnuts.

"You need to get these shelled in the next few days or they won't be as good," she'd said. "Get your little marmots to help you, my dear. You might as well get some work out of them." When I thanked her she muttered, "It'll keep those monkeys quiet for a few hours if nothing else." I'd laughed to myself. At least I was getting a good workout in French. My tutor would be pleased.

Scripture still seemed to have a scratchiness to it, itching me so much that I'd have to put the Bible down and find something else to do, absolutely anything! I'd retreat to clean the kitchen, disappointed in myself, and I'd hear the clock ticking, my metronome. The words from a hymn would sneak into my head, "There's within my heart a melody; Jesus whispers sweet and low, Fear not, I am with thee, peace, be still, In all of life's ebb and flow . . . " The next thing I knew, I'd be humming it—or outright singing along with the clock.

It was strange. I kept thinking of Jessie's heaven, the flea market, and how I'd felt God's presence among the strangers there as they manhandled crosses and statues of saints. God wasn't just there. The last time I'd walked Sammy through the public park downtown, the lush growth seemed to nearly throb with God, vibrating out of the soil, springing up through the blades of grass, through the cedar trees and the rosebuds, pulsing God into the air, against my eardrums. Jardin Lecoq was a green cathedral, yet Christ Church Auvergne was just another building. How could that be?

I'd think more on that this morning. I'd planned to take Sam downtown anyway: he needed new shoes now that it was too chilly for socks and sandals. Before the stores opened we'd stroll around the cathedral for a little while. I always felt close to God there. Maybe it was the mystery of the place, reminding me that I didn't need to have everything figured out. Or maybe it was the size of the cathedral itself. Walking into the sanctuary was like wading into the deep end of an enormous pool. There was so much God there, working into my pores, my soul.

I did a quick coffee with the ladies first, but the discussion topic got stuck in who was moving home in December and where they'd found a house, and how nice it'd be to have fast food drive-throughs again and banks with pneumatic tubes. I made my excuses and left early.

Place de la Victoire was deserted. As we neared the cathedral I saw none of the usual faithful flocking to the doors, not even the beggar woman parked by the side entrance, her back hunched and hand outstretched, or the skinhead punks sitting under the eaves, yelling at passersby for money. Maybe the gendarmes had swept the grounds of them or it was too cold or too early. Whatever the case, I was glad to be nearly alone with Sam as we walked closer, listening to my thoughts, the brush of a broom from the street sweeper, the warbles of the pigeons, and the clink and clank of the lady outside the brasserie unstacking the café chairs.

"We're going into the big church," I said to Sam, handing him his favorite toy of the moment, the plastic cow from his barnyard set. "We have to be quiet."

Sam nestled back in his stroller, kicking his feet and slobbering on the cow.

I stepped into the cathedral and adjusted my eyes to the dim light. How I loved that smell. It said I'm older than anything you know or understand.

I tried to walk softly. The slightest tap on the stone floor reverberated 100 feet up to the vaulted ceiling, and I didn't want to disturb the few people scattered in the individual chapels in the back, lighting candles, or kneeling in prayer. The light streamed through the stained glass windows in great shafts, stirring the dust in swirls around the hundreds of empty chairs sitting before the vacant pulpit, like ghost parishioners.

I approached the altar, now roped off, and remembered Madame Pink Suit offering me the bread in my dream.

Remember, God? I've given you the key. I've taken the bread. I'm ready to do whatever you want. Just ask.

I pulled Sam's stroller beside me, sat down amid the hundreds of empty chairs, and prayed silently, my eyes open, watching Sam finger his toy. I prayed for Cindy, who'd be leaving at Christmas. Then I built up to the big question, the one that had been on my heart for weeks now: What could I do to recapture our old two-way relationship, the one where I served and read scripture and tried my best to follow Jesus, and God was present with me in the serving and the reading?

I knew I'd prayed to let go of normal, and I'd done that in every other area of my life and it was wonderful. But I still wished that my faith would be like it had always been—where I could sense just the least little bit that I was earning God's love, even though he gave it away for free. I wanted to be the child of God I used to be—not the kind who's always embarrassing herself, then hiding behind her mother's legs, but the hardworking child, the one who people see and pat God on the shoulder and say, "What a nice girl and, my, how she favors you!"

It was hard to ask God for anything at all. I was so grateful to be plucked out of my ordinary former life and set down in this wonderland, however crazy it could be at times. But I had to ask.

"Jou mama, jou," Sam broke in. I didn't have juice. While I searched my tote bag for a sippy cup of water, he discovered his echo and tried it again and again. Finally I found the cup and plugged his mouth with it. He sipped, made a face, and threw it against a chair. An old woman turned around to look.

I handed it back, and he threw it again. We'd have to go.

Which door should we take? The cathedral was so big that I couldn't remember which one led back to Place de la Victoire. I picked an exit, pulled the stroller out backwards so the huge door wouldn't slam on us, turned around and gasped at the view. I had never been there before, perched high above the flight of steps leading down to rue des Gras, the cobblestone pedestrian street that seemed to unroll like a carpet down the hill, through the city, and back up again to the green mountains in the distance and all the way to the Puy de Dôme. It was the right street, but I'd never get Sam's stroller down all those steps.

Don't go yet. Look.

I could take another minute to enjoy the scenery. I'd seen antique postcards at the flea market of that quartier a hundred years earlier and it still looked exactly the same, the same medieval stone buildings with their shutters and red tiled roofs, the same eyebrow of stones curving over the windows, the same: terra cotta chimney pots on the roof tops and cobblestone street below, and above the second floor window of the building on the right the same amazing bas relief of Christ washing the feet of the disciples, carved right into the lava stone wall. Did people ever notice it? Did the street sweeper who worked there every day? Did the little old ladies making their way up the hill to the church?

I was about to go back inside and try another door when I caught a blur of movement on the street out of the corner of my eye. It was Pale Lady, the prostitute who always hung around downtown, clicking across the cobblestones in her thigh-high boots toward the *tabac*. Sarah had christened her Pale Lady the first time she saw her on account of her frizzy curls of white-blond hair, her pale skin, and white lipstick. "She looks like an angel," Sarah said, and I gave Todd a look.

A few weeks ago when I was walking downtown with the coffee

ladies, Pale Lady had stopped me on the street and asked me for a light. I'd stood there trying to explain to her that I don't smoke, struggling for the word for matches, until Barbara grabbed me by the arm and said to come on. Didn't I know that she was one of the town prostitutes? Besides, I was standing in the bus lane. Was it really worth Sam and me getting flattened by a bus just to be polite?

As gaunt as Pale Lady was, I'd assumed she was a beggar and probably an addict. A few days later as we walked downtown with the kids, she stopped us outside Marché St. Pierre and asked Todd for money for coffee. He gave her the change in his pocket as I led the kids into the market. I really didn't want her to bother me again this morning. Maybe she'd be gone by the time I pushed Sam around.

She wasn't.

She stood in a shaft of sunlight next to the jewelry store, smoking a cigarette. I groaned. She's going to ask me for money, and I spent my last ten francs on coffee. I probably had more in the bottom of my purse, but I didn't want to stand there looking for it while the café lady watched us, smirking that Pale Lady had conned another foreigner into giving her some change.

I flattened my smile into a line as I approached her, removing any sparkle from my eyes. It was almost natural to me now to put on the bored face the French give to strangers on the street. It was depressing. but it had helped me fit in. I pushed the stroller past Pale Lady, being careful to avoid eye contact. At the exact moment when I could have chosen to say hello or to give her a friendly nod, Sam lurched forward and started babbling at her. I marched on and he twisted himself to look behind the stroller, reaching back for something.

Was she following me? I could see her approach out of the corner of my eye. Sam was reaching to her!

"Maa!" he called and tried to wriggle out of his seat as I jerked to the right. What was she doing?

"Madame, madame," she called.

I walked faster.

What did she want? Why wouldn't weird people ever leave me alone? I'd already been accosted by a drunken man near school, and just the other day at a public playground a creepy man in a trench coat had patted the front of his pants and suggested we go enjoy each other at his apartment.

"Madame," she called again, and I heard her boots clicking closer behind me. She was running after me? Was she trying to intimidate me into giving her money?

She reached for my arm.

I spun around and barked, "*Laissez moi tranquille*! (Leave me alone!)"

Time stopped as she stared back at me with glassy eyes of the faintest blue. Her right eye twitched. She reached for my hand and pressed Sam's little plastic cow into my palm with her bony fingers.

"He dropped it," she said. "It's too dirty now for the baby."

She turned and clicked up the hill. Stunned, my eyes met those of the café lady. She pretended not to notice and started sweeping again.

"Merci, madame," I called after Pale Lady. She kept walking.

All she had wanted to do was to help me, and I had run from her. I had run from her! She'd probably remembered that I was a foreigner and that any conversation with me was bound to be awkward, but she'd tried to help me anyway. In the months since our move I'd had a half-dozen clerks hear my accent and disappear to the back of the store, preferring to hide than have an awkward conversation. But she had sought me out, for a silly toy cow.

Was this some kind of message from God, a modern-day parable to show me how self-righteous I was, so focused on reclaiming my closeness to God? She was trying to serve me, and I would not have it—me, the one who wanted to serve.

I pushed the stroller back up the street toward the cathedral, hoping I could find her and say thank you, but she was gone. A bird flew in front of my face, soaring past the foot-washing scene in the wall I'd admired a few minutes before: Jesus, washing the feet of the disciples. My heart lurched. Pale Lady had bent before me too.

I fingered the toy cow in my jacket pocket. Something about that moment when she grabbed my hand and pressed it into my palm felt oddly familiar, as if I'd been there before. I pushed the stroller off the curb and remembered. I had been there before—sort of, though in a dream, when Madame Pink Suit pressed the bread into my palm, saying, "Take, eat." Pale Lady had tried to serve me as well.

I spent the afternoon at home, moving from chore to chore in silence, save for Sam's blabbering and the tick of my clock. The lovely comtoise comforted me, swinging off the minutes from her corner, humming me a lullaby. In her gentle rocking I could dare to ask myself some serious questions.

While I'd been so absorbed with my own search for God, had I shut others out of my life? I'd let in Jessie and Cindy to a point, but I had judged them, wondering and measuring if they were spiritual enough or Christian enough. Who was I to determine anything about anyone else?

Forgive me, God.

After I brought the kids home from school and started them on their homework, I hid in the kitchen and started dinner. As usual, the chicken I'd bought at Eco Marché still had tiny feathers that needed plucking. I took out the pair of tweezers I had bought just for this task and began plucking the feathers, one by one. The mindless gesture felt a little like penitence, like fingering a rosary bead.

As I plucked, I dreamed up a saint card just for Pale Lady. I'd draw her with her white curls, her pale skin, and white lipstick, as she bent before me, pressing the toy cow into my hands. Her face and her outstretched hand would take up most of the card, with her big eyes searching into mine, her bony fingers on my baby's toy.

The tagline?

Jesus' hands.

I repeated the prayer as I plucked each feather:

Forgive me, God, and open me to others. Open my heart up wide, big enough for a bus to drive in. Flatten me, God, with openness.

Chapter 11

Passing of the Peace, Flea Market Style

Jessie was supposed to meet me at nine o'clock by the entrance to the Champion grocery store for another flea market Sunday morning. But after a half hour of waiting, trying to look nonchalant as the man on the curb drinking a bottle of wine from a paper bag kept looking me over as if I were a croissant, I crossed the street to go back to my car.

Sorry, God, I prayed. I still want to be open, but maybe not to him.

I was almost back to my car when a white Opal idling in a city drive-way blocked the sidewalk. An old lady in church clothes had gotten out to fasten her gate behind it. She motioned me to step into her courtyard to cross, and I smiled and nodded a thank you. How sad that someone had sprayed graffiti all over the corner of her house. I glanced into her courtyard and nearly lost my breath. Someone had painted a lemon tree on the wall inside, and the lawn was a gorgeous checkerboard of grass and brick. There was a fountain in the center flanked by two potted topiaries of roses, still in bloom. All that, hidden behind a gate and graffiti!

I was so overcome that I tripped on a rise in the sidewalk. I'd just found my footing when a loud creaking startled me from across the street. A girl was opening her metal shutters. As she folded them back against the wall, a cat leapt out of her apartment onto the window ledge.

I unlocked my car and had just put the key in the ignition when suddenly both sides of the street surged with more movement, the front doors opening, one after another, the men and women walking out, as if they'd planned it, like a scene out of a musical! I half expected them to spin each other into the air and break into song. Everything was opening up, all at the same time.

I'd prayed for God to open me to others, and life was giving me a visual aide. The whole world was opening to me, waiting for me to make the next move.

As the old lady in the Opal drove past, I turned to see her gate closed. If I hadn't looked at the right moment I would have just seen the graffiti, with no idea of the wonderland behind it.

Take time to look, my fairy godmother clock whispered in my ears. Take time.

I certainly had plenty of that. I had an embarrassment of time. I'd hidden it from everyone back home when they asked me how I spent my days. How could I tell them I lolled through my life like a child, puttering and playing? But now the world was inviting me—or maybe God was calling me—to put aside my instincts to be stingy and throw my time around a little, like the rich Monopoly man in his top hat, tossing out hundred dollar bills.

Why on earth was I retreating back home? If I needed to throw around my time a little, the flea market was the perfect place to start.

As I followed the man with his dog, backtracking past the graffiti, I drew in my jacket and adjusted the purse on my shoulder. Don't go crazy, I heard my mother say. You're all by yourself.

I joined the masses, and someone bumped me from behind. I hugged my purse tighter. Caught in a sudden squeeze of people, it was too late to turn around. A burly man going in the opposite direction pressed up against me, his chest against mine, breathing his morning breath on me. I turned my head, "Pardon," I said, and he muttered something to the old man beside him, not even noticing me. They aren't trying to intimidate, I told myself. Be open. Be brave.

The knot of people loosened, and I walked freely now among the hundreds of people—the beautiful nobodies, the men unshaven, the women unadorned with makeup; busy shaking hands, exchanging kisses, bargaining, and joking with one another. How had I'd missed this with Cindy and Jessie? I'd been so dazzled by the range of holy things that I'd missed the sparks of human connection going off all around me.

As I walked through the web of handshakes and kisses amid tables stacked high with the detritus of people's lives, there was a definite Presence breathing over all of us. It felt strange, this connection I'd never noticed before. The mere existence of the people shouted God's presence to me, and even their things seemed to speak God's name, as if that made sense! It was as if the sheets and the teapots and the books rose up and cried out for the people there and the people long gone who'd slept under them or sipped from them or turned their pages, saying, "I was here!" "God loved me too."

An hour later I was lost in the faces of the people, having forgotten all about pickpockets or leering eyes. I was watching an old lady behind a table of saint statues, smoking a cigarette and bracing herself against the chill, when a man darted in front of me, nearly making me trip. I waited for him to say pardon, but he just scowled and then picked his nose. Didn't he have a handkerchief in that big bag of his? I watched as he leaned over her table, muttering to himself. He picked up a girl saint (another Saint Anne?) and put it back again, knocking over two more. As he walked off, spitting onto the pavement, the vendor sighed and shook her head.

The woman gently righted the saints, lining them up as if they were waiting at a bus stop, and I laughed, imagining Jesus driving up and letting them all climb in. Jessie was right. They were lovely—regal yet meek, lovely though chipped and worn, shabby as the shoppers who walked by. It seemed sad to leave them there, the smoke from the vendor's cigarette descending onto their heads in dirty halos. Jessie would have rescued them.

It was nearly half past eleven already. I'd walk the aisle and then head home. The next table was laden with all sorts of junk, the ubiquitous ashtrays and an obscene nut cracker shaped like a lady. The man beside me was examining it, laughing to his girlfriend, "See, you put the nut in her something (crotch?) and snap, crack it open." The woman laughed and I looked away, my eyes landing on a gilded frame. The baptismal certificate! I reached to pick it up, and a hand with dirty fingernails moved over mine—the weasel man.

"Well, well. The American girl is back! And how are you today?"

I felt a sudden pang of self-consciousness. I'd kept my mouth closed all morning, keeping the secret to myself that I wasn't one of them, looking and listening, enjoying my place as an adult in the crowd—not a foreigner with toddler French. My heart skipped a beat. Be bold and brave like Jessie.

"I'm fine, thank you. How much is this, monsieur?"

"Where is your tall friend?"

Why was he asking that? Did he want to see if I was on my own so he could pull something over on me?

"Over there," I lied, nodding across the parking lot. "How much is this, please?"

"Eighty-five francs, madame," and then he went into a long explanation of why it was so expensive.

Expensive . . . ? What was that—fourteen dollars? It was someone's sacred treasure, the record of their wedding to God, and he was practically giving it away. Did I have that much? I looked to see.

The weasel-faced man bounced a cigarette in his lips and smiled as I searched. "You like it, don't you? You liked it last week, and here you are again."

"Yes, monsieur."

"So why are you here?"

"Pardon?"

"Oh my dear, no, I don't mean to offend you. I'm very happy that you're here. I only want to know what brings you to France. It is my curiosity. I am a very curious man."

An old woman stopped browsing to watch me. "My husband works for Michelin," I stuttered, wishing I could disappear. I pictured it atop a mound of trash at the déchetterie. "I have a question, please."

"So do I," he said. "Your husband makes you happy?"

The man beside him elbowed him and laughed. "Leave her alone, Maurice," he said. "Don't mind him," he whispered. "He's a playboy."

"I can't help myself," the weasel man said. "Beautiful women are my weakness."

Beautiful women? He was talking about me? He was laughing, amused with me. The woman folded her arms and chuckled.

"Would you take sixty francs?" I asked, my heart beating in my ears.

"How about seventy?"

"I have only sixty-five, sir," I said, and pulled the money out to show him.

"Well . . . OK, madame," he said, "for sixty-five . . . and a smile."

Shocked, I made a face.

"That's not it," he said. The woman cackled.

I felt myself blush and couldn't help smiling.

"That wasn't so hard, was it?" he said as I turned away.

"Merci, monsieur."

"You come back. And bring your tall friend."

I walked quickly back down the aisle, adrenaline pumping, holding tightly to the treasure of little René Ducout, a boy from another world and time, now a part of my life. He would be . . . what, ninety years old, if he were still alive?

I looked into the faces of the strangers walking past, oddly aware as the sleeves of their jackets brushed by mine, as I smelled their cologne, as we exchanged places in the aisle. I'd prayed, "Open the door to others for me, God," and life answered me with the old lady's gate, the dog at the door, and the weasel man. The doors were already open, not merely cracked but flung wide, waiting for me.

The doors of Église St. Thomas were open too. As I walked past the church on the way to my car, I listened for the singing but didn't hear any. Maybe they were in prayer or the priest was giving his sermon. I walked on, waiting for the wistfulness to descend, the "why can't I connect with God?" but it wasn't there. I felt only a quiet satisfaction within me, knowing I'd somehow had my own passing of the peace there in the parking lot with all those beautiful nobodies. Was this crazy? Who knew whether they believed in God or cared if God exists, but the peace I felt that God was moving among them was as tangible as René Ducout's certificate in my hands.

Would I find that same peace at my own church that night?

Ten minutes into worship, it felt to me as if God had once been there, but then gathered his things and ditched us. It was probably my own fault. We got to church late after turning the house upside down looking for Ben's shoes, and barely made it into the pew before the opening hymn. I looked around at the congregation. Did they notice anything different? Everyone seemed perfectly content, as if this was exactly what they expected from church. It must have been me.

Father Joe paused to clear his throat—just a little cough, nothing to warrant my sudden compulsion to stand up, put my purse on my shoulder, and walk down the aisle and right out the chapel doors. What was wrong with me?

I pulled Sam onto my lap to serve as my anchor, to weigh me down as my daydreams drifted up to the ceiling. Baby Sam reached forward and grabbed my shirt, hoisting himself to a standing position. He bounced up and down, babbling so loudly that the entire congregation started to snicker. What happened to Todd taking over Sam duty? I shot him a look and Todd smiled at me, so I shot him another one.

"Oh, sorry," he mouthed, and pulled Sam onto his lap. Todd let him amuse himself by pulling things out of the diaper bag and tossing them onto the floor. I tried to ignore it but when Sam found one of my nursing pads and waved it around like a flag, I couldn't take it anymore. I snatched it away, took a deep breath, and looked at Jesus in the stained glass window.

Please God, just a little help here? I'm trying. I really am.

Minutes later, as I waited in line for communion, my brain started playing a hymn from home in my head: "Fear not I am with thee, peace, be still, in all of life's ebb and flow." Yes, I know God is with me. I had no doubt of that. I could hear Sam crying in the back pew with Todd, calling me back. I heard a moped in the distance and thought of Madame Pink Suit, beckoning me out. Church went on, but every sound seemed to call me down the aisle and out the open door, back to the market, back to the people of God.

The people of God . . . ? I knew that calling them that was odd, but that's what came to me. My newest saints deserved a card of their own. I'd draw them as I saw them in my mind, beckoning me to join them from behind an iron gate. They'd all be there, even René Ducout stepping out of 1919, a boy, a child, to lead the throng. Jesus would like that. There would be the weasel man, the lady with the bus stop of saints, even the man picking his nose—all of them.

Swirly letters would announce the caption:

The People of God

The prayer?

God, whose spirit falls on whomever it chooses, help us see you and feel your presence with holy nobodies, as we all are. Thank you for being a God who dances in a top hat, tossing us all surprise blessings, whether we line up for you or not. When we fall or are knocked down, gently right us. Help us listen to the instinct you put within us to get up and follow you through open doors, no matter where they lead.

But what if the doors led me away from church? God wouldn't lead me away, surely.

As everyone put on their coats, some kids opened the chapel door and the rain blew in, scattering stray programs and soaking the entrance. I hurried over to close the door but left it open a crack, looking out into the church yard. *L'automne* was here to stay, I thought, pulling Sam onto my hip. The trees were yellowing, the flowers crinkled up and brown. Everything green might be starting to die, but the earth still seemed furiously alive to me, calling me out of the little stone chapel and into the beautiful rain.

Chapter 12
The Cup of Salvation

I hung René Ducout's baptismal certificate next to the clock in my living room, and with every swing of her pendulum, my fairy godmother seemed to motion me over for a closer look. I'd stand beside her and admire each one of her illustrated scenes—well, almost each one.

I loved Mary with her crown, Joseph with his lily, and the angel Gabriel with his hand pointing skyward. I loved the three vignettes of the sacraments: the rites of baptism, first communion, and confirmation. And of course I loved the scenes of Jesus, the large one in the middle breaking the bread and the portrait at the top. There was one scene, however, that got under my skin.

It was my friend, my very first saint, Joan of Arc gazing at a portrait of Jesus, clutching her sword to her breast. She was still following me through my life in France, making herself at home in my wallet, as Jessie's Siamese twin, at the high school that bore her name next to École St. Pierre, and now from the certificate. I admired her devotion, of course, but she had an irritating way of reminding me of what I was trying to ignore: my own lack of useful service.

What was I doing to serve my savior? Eating éclairs and going shopping and drinking coffee with the ladies? Nice. Whenever my eyes drifted to Joan on the certificate, I'd guide them back to Jesus, focusing on his hands. They were lovely, even with the scars. I liked his right hand best, the way he raised it with his fingers relaxed, as if he was saying, "By the way, I just thought of something you should know."

Sunday came around again, but there'd be no flea market for me today. While my neighbors lingered over their breakfast tables, drinking their coffee in the lamplight, my early bird husband was rounding us up, pestering us into rain jackets and then into the car. "Didn't you people say you wanted to have some fun?" he said as he buckled Sam into his car seat. "You'll see. It'll be the best Sunday ever."

I winced. The best Sunday ever . . . ? Without church?

Ben spoke up. "But I miss what we used to do on Sunday mornings."

I tried not to look shocked. "That's so sweet, Ben," I said. "You know, sometimes I miss First Baptist too."

"What are you talking about?" Ben said. "I miss the part like last Sunday where you go to the flea market and we get to stay home in our pajamas."

Almost an hour later the five of us stood in raincoats in the middle of a street staring at a foot-and-a-half-long earthworm. Ben knelt down beside it, gently nudging it with a twig he'd picked up. "If the worms are this big, I can't wait to see the apples!"

We'd see plenty of apples, no question. The tiny village of Ludesse was having the annual Foire à la Pomme, its apple festival. No wonder Todd had pushed us to go. We never missed the apple festival in Hendersonville, North Carolina. It was a fall ritual of ours.

"Quit, Ben," Sarah said. "You're bothering it."

"I'm not bothering it," Ben said. "I'm helping it." As it started to wiggle onto the stick, a Frenchman carrying an empty basket walked up and peered down over our shoulders.

"Ah," he said. "I've never seen one that large . . . very impressive."

A Peugeot quickly approached behind us, and we hurried the children out of the road. "But the worm . . ." Ben said.

The car straddled it.

"Whew!" Sarah said. "That was close."

Before anyone could answer or walk closer, a truck barreled through, the tires slicing the worm in half.

Ben stood with his mouth open.

"Too bad," said the man, shrugging his shoulders. He walked with us closer to inspect the wriggling halves. "Now that size," he said, pointing to one half with his shoe, "that size I've seen before." He walked on ahead of us, whistling.

We followed him through the drizzle into town. Music played from the loudspeakers, and occasionally a man's voice interrupted, inviting people to . . . something, something, something. While I was trying to decipher the French, a bicycle bell rang behind us. A boy whipped around the corner, nearly running us over with a push cart loaded with crates of apples. The cart had orange crepe paper woven through the spokes of its wheels, balloons taped all over the sides, and a white poster board in the back covered with pictures of different kinds of apples.

"Excuse us, please. Delivery coming through. Let us by," called the boy, ringing the bell on the handle again, as a lady with an umbrella walked behind them, getting her keys out of her purse, telling the boy that hers was the blue Citroen.

The streets were crowded, despite the soft rain. Apple vendors had set up under tents and umbrellas on each side of the narrow road, interspersed with the regular market goods—cheese, spices, tablecloths, knives. We walked along with the crowd, occasionally making way for another boy with an apple cart.

"Why is it just for boys?" Sarah asked, and just then a little girl's voice called from behind, *"Excusez-moi s'il vous plaît."* She was pushing a cart decorated with ivy and tissue paper flowers, the colors dribbling down the wagon in the rain.

The wind gently blew against us as we walked past stacked stone houses, the shutters open, showing off the lace curtains on the windows and geraniums, now leggy in the flowerboxes. The air smelled of rain, wet dog, coffee, and *merguez* sausage and onions from a sidewalk stand. Ben asked to stop and look at the pocket knives for sale, and Sam reached up and pulled the tent above the table, sending a trickle of water down the back of Todd's neck.

"Hey up there," Todd said, and reached up to grab Sam's hands, which threw Sam into giggles. The knife man chuckled at Sam and offered Todd a cloth to dry himself. Sarah and I walked ahead to look at a table full of wooden clogs. The redhead behind the table put out her cigarette and explained how the shoes were made.

There were stories behind everything—the hand-carved wooden spoons, dried herbs in little baggies, giant wheels of cheese, fresh butter, and thick brown loaves of country bread dusty with flour. There was even an artist talking about his work—sunny canvases of meadows and poppies and the lavender fields of Provence. As we ate our lunch on the side of the road, watching chickens peck around someone's front yard,

I wished I could have a painting of that very day, complete with the drizzle and tents and chickens.

"This isn't exactly a hot dog," Ben said, gnawing off big bites of the baguette stuffed with a merguez sausage and oily French fries.

"But it's not bad," Sarah said, pulling her fries out to eat them separately. "Can we have dessert?" There were plenty of choices: sugared nuts, *barbe á papa* ("Papa's beard," cotton candy), and of course candy apples—*pommes d'amour*, literally translated "love apples." Love apples! I bought one for Todd and one for me, and promptly cut my lip trying to bite into the red candy glass. I guess love hurts sometimes.

The rain began to pour, and we ran into an open garage where a group of men were crowded around tables set with bottles and cups, drinking and talking quietly. Was this OK, to barge into someone's small garage uninvited? There was a lady with a cash box and prices listed for the different wines, which answered my question.

"Do you want some?" Todd asked. "I'm going to have a glass of red. It looks like they've got cider."

I was all for being open, but wine at ten o'clock in the morning?

"I'll take cider," I said, imagining cinnamon sticks and brown sugar.

Todd brought me a bowl with liquid in it.

"You drink it out of a bowl?"

Todd nodded.

"It's not hot," I said, looking it over. It was golden—and fizzy. I wrinkled my nose. "It smells like apple juice gone bad."

"Try it, Beck. I had some at Jean Luc's. You'll love it."

A loud pop came from the back of the room. A burly man with a big mustache took a cloth and wiped the neck of a bottle.

"That's your cider," Todd said. "The cork pops like champagne."

"I want some," Ben said. "Can I have a little?"

"No," I said, lifting it to my mouth. "It's not Champomy. It has alcohol in it."

"Are you going to get drunk?"

"Benjamin Ramsey," Sarah scolded. "Of course she's not. Mommy doesn't get drunk. She's just going to taste it."

"Cider doesn't have much alcohol in it, anyway," Todd said. "Three percent, I think. Maybe less."

Ben and Sarah stood watching me, as if I were about to transform into Mr. Hyde.

I brought the bowl to my lips. The fizzy nectar swirled over my tongue with light sweetness, bubbles! It was heaven! Joy! Apples made this when they soured? This was too amazing!

I opened my eyes to see Ben and Sarah still staring at me. "Look, the rain has stopped," I said, trying to distract them. I took a big sip. It was so delicious that I had to force myself to slow down. I could have downed the whole bowl in one big gulp. It was heaven, sweetness, light!

A sudden wind fluttered my damp hair. The gray clouds had moved aside, and big beams of sunlight were streaming through, flooding the wet streets. I took another long gulp. . . . Heavenly goodness, sweet heavenly goodness. I liked apples, but this? This was divine!

"I'm guessing you like it," Todd said.

"Can't I just have one sip?" Ben asked.

"Ben, be quiet and drink your Coke," Sarah said, eying me suspiciously.

"Sarah, what's that face for?" I asked, wanting to yell out, "This is the most incredible thing I've ever tasted in my whole entire life!"

"It's basically just apple juice." I said, patting her back. "I'd forgotten how good apple juice is."

I returned my bowl to a lady at a table in the back who plunked it into sudsy dishwater, and we walked into the sunshine, right into the path of a roving band of men in traditional costume: wide-brimmed hats, blue smocks, red kerchiefs tied around their necks, as they played the accordion, a hand-cranked hurdy-gurdy, and what looked to be some sort of bagpipe.

As the kids watched I whispered to Todd, "Do you think we could go back and buy a bottle of that cider?"

"If you want, but they sell it in all the grocery stores too."

"It's in the grocery stores?!"

I was rethinking my complaints about the wasted space in our house of a wine cave when Ben interrupted. "Mama, look at the parade! Clowns!"

A troop of adults wearing long green robes stood talking to each other. They wore medals hanging from wide red ribbons around their necks, and a bearded man was holding a banner that read, "*Confrérie de la Pomme.*" Brotherhood of the Apple . . . ? Was it some kind of apple growers' organization . . . a Rotary Club?

"I don't think they're clowns, Ben," Sarah observed.

"If they are," he said, "they're not very good at it."

Before we left, we bought a crate of apples. All the kids pushing carts were busy, so we hired Ben and Sarah to haul them back to the car. They were moving along fine until they saw the inflatable moonwalk. An enterprising mom had set it up in her front yard and made a sign, **10 minutes for 10 francs.** As I fumbled in my purse for a dix franc, she yelled at her children, "Get out right this minute and let the foreign children in!"

"Non, non," I said. "It's not necessary. Let them finish." But she insisted, and her children quickly climbed out and stood beside it, pressing their faces against the screen, giggling at my kids' English and mimicking it to each other.

Todd and I stood against her stone fence and smiled at each other. The ivy clinging in all the nooks and crannies of the fence had turned from red to purple. The sun was still shining.

Would the kids miss me if I ran back to the cider stand for another bowl?

"I knew you'd like the cider," Todd said.

Was he reading my mind? "I don't think I've ever had anything I liked better."

"It's been a nice Sunday," Todd said.

"It's been a perfect Sunday," I added as I felt a sudden twinge of guilt. A perfect Sunday and we hadn't even thought about Christ Church—or any church. Back in South Carolina we'd be rushing to church, rushing home, rushing to the grocery store or a birthday party or a soccer tournament or out for school supplies before class on Monday. We'd played the day away like kids, and yet I'd felt a holy presence and peace all day long.

"I don't want it to end," I said to Todd, as the kids put on their shoes.

"It doesn't have to. Let's take a drive by Murol on the way home."

Ben cheered. We'd been to Château Murol once before, back before Ben started his collection of castle toilet photos. The fifteenth-century castle had several, and now he'd have a camera to document them.

"I wish every Sunday could be like today," Sarah said as we made our way through the countryside. I looked out the window at the hills, tempting me. Every Sunday could be just like this one if we chose it to be that way. We didn't have to go to church. Cindy and Tom had made that choice, and we could too if we wanted to do it. Christ Church wasn't our denomination anyway. We could always have our own services at home.

But I wanted church to be a part of our lives—for myself, for the kids. They needed to keep learning about God, the sacred stories in the Bible, how important it is to pray and to gather with fellow believers, about being obedient, even when you're not in the mood. Besides, everyone else in my family liked Christ Church fine, and the other expats raved about it.

Still, last week in the pew I could practically feel myself wilt. The light illuminating the stained glass Jesus should have reminded me of his presence in the chapel, but instead it seemed to flaunt what was beyond the walls, saying, "See what's out there? Let me show it to you!"

But we couldn't stop going, no matter how I felt about the services. I couldn't skip out on church.

We pulled into the gravel lot outside Château Murol. Where was everyone? Was it closed? The gate was locked tight. Todd indulged Ben, lending him the camera to snap away at the castle toilets, and then we trudged back down the hill.

"Look who's waiting for us," Todd said.

It was Jacques, the donkey, whom our kids had named the last time we were here, braying at us from the field across the castle grounds.

"Do you want a juicy red apple, Jacques?" Ben said, running to the fence, waving his half-eaten apple. Foamy green drool started dripping out of the donkey's mouth.

"Gross," said Ben, pulling the apple back, as Jacques came close.

"Don't tease him," Todd said. "Look how he wants it. Show him he can trust you."

Ben held out his hand with the apple and Jacques mouthed it, turning it over in Ben's hand.

"Yuck! His lips are hairy!" Jacques ate the whole thing, core and all, as we laughed and cheered him on.

Sarah ran back to the car for more apples, and I followed behind her with the keys, overwhelmed by a quiet joy. The sun was shining, and I felt like Jacques, drooling at all that God held out for me in this beautiful French life: the preciousness of time, the holiness of strangers, and the sacredness of a bowl of cider shared in a stranger's garage.

My next holy card came easily:

The Cup of Salvation

I'd draw the cider the way it was, fizzy and golden, in a simple bowl, cradled in my hands. I'd label it "The Cup of Salvation," not on account of its heavenly taste—although it truly was divine—but because it transported me to the altar table, standing in someone's humble garage, among others as undeserving as any of us. I drank in its symbolism: that the cider maker and God had taken ordinary apples, pressed them, added their own sweetness, and then let time take its course. What once were apples would fall apart into something beautiful and new.

The prayer was mine:

> Press me, God. Blend in me your love and light. Let me fall apart into something beautiful and new. Pour me out and hold me in the cup of your hands. May I be pleasing to you.

It was tempting to put my hopes for church aside and be content with more days like this, letting God work on me wherever I found myself. But it didn't seem right to shut the door to being with God in his own house of worship. I would keep forcing my feet in the pew, week after week, and the fog would break eventually. I just needed to get myself there and wriggle through the hour a few minutes at a time, like the foot-and-a-half-long worm making its way across the road. Hopefully a truck wasn't hidden around the bend.

Chapter 13

Gleaning

When I picked up the phone and heard Father Joe's voice on the line Tuesday evening, my heart leapt and relief swept in. At last he was going to ask me to serve in some way! What would it be? Read scripture? Take up the offering? Teach Sunday School or help with communion? I tried not to sound too eager. We enjoyed a little small talk, and then he said he had something to ask me.

"Sure," I said calmly, as if I hadn't expected a thing. This was it!

"Could I please speak to Todd?"

Really, Lord? This was how it was going to be?

I handed my husband the phone, crossed my arms and stood there, listening to the one-sided conversation.

"How about that?" Todd chirped, hanging up. "He wants me to do the Old Testament reading on Sunday."

"You're kidding me."

Todd eyed me nervously.

"I don't get it," I said. "I just told Father Joe at the end of the last service that I'd be glad to help."

Had I sent out a conflicting message with my body language or tone of voice? And anyway, where was God in this? Father Joe might have just forgotten, but couldn't God help me out a little? Hadn't I promised that I would wriggle along on my belly like a worm, refusing to give up on Christ Church, no matter how tempting last Sunday had been? We'd had such a delicious time, wandering around the apple festival, moving on to Murol when we felt like it, completely free. I hadn't even considered leaving Christ Church, sure that a breakthrough was just around the corner. And now this!

As much as I knew God would never shut me out, it felt a little personal.

"Becky, I'm sure Father Joe didn't mean to overlook you. He probably just got busy and forgot. Look, you can take my place if you want," Todd said. "You're a better reader than I am anyway."

"No, no," I answered. "He asked you. That's fine. It's no big deal."

On Saturday night I tried to help Todd by looking up the passage in Ruth for him to read over, thinking he might want to practice. I was glad to do it. I could tell the story of Ruth in my sleep: how Ruth clings to her mother-in-law Naomi after both of their husbands die, how she follows her back to her homeland, knowing they'll face poverty and an uncertain future. I loved the image of Ruth in Boaz's field, following behind the harvesters, gleaning it of the leftover wheat to take back to Naomi. I'd even considered using the Song of Ruth ("Entreat Me Not to Leave Thee") for our wedding. I loved that story, and I wasn't sure how well Todd knew it.

"Don't you want to glance over it?" I asked, offering him the Bible.

"Thanks," Todd said, "but I'll just look it over once we get there."

Todd's reading went fine, except for the loud scuffling in our pew as Sam tried to wrestle out of my arms to join his daddy at the pulpit. I thought Sam might settle down once Todd returned to his seat, but he spent the rest of the hour babbling loudly and pulling on Ben. "I'll take him," Todd said, but Todd let Sam make faces at the kids behind us, getting them in trouble. Finally I couldn't take it anymore and took Sam back to the children's area. He stormed around like a wild man, sucking on toys I'd never seen before.

When it was time for communion I pulled Sam on my hip and got in line. Ben and Sarah gave me pleading glances from their place in the pew, but I shook my head. It was hard enough to manage Sam. Did they have to keep begging me to let them bend the rules? They heard the priest. Communion was open to all who were baptized, and that didn't include them, no matter how many times they told me it wasn't fair. Communion wasn't a mindless ritual. They needed to wait until it meant something. Todd didn't make it any easier, shrugging his shoulders whenever they asked him about it.

As the line moved forward, I watched Mary Margaret near the front of the line. At the last couple of services I'd noticed that she always made the sign of the cross before stepping forward to the table.

I'd seen people do that on television, and it always fascinated me. Now I wondered how it felt and what it meant.

It was her turn. She approached the altar table, and I watched as she touched her forehead first, then her stomach, then her right and left shoulders. How beautiful, to physically draw a cross against her body and honor the Trinity as she took the bread and cup. Why didn't Baptists do that? It was too ritualistic, most likely. How many times had I been warned about the danger of getting so used to certain practices—the Lord's Supper, the Lord's prayer—that we get attached to the ritual rather than what it stands for? I could see where people could make the sign out of habit, but I still wished I could do it, to say to God as I neared his table, "I am yours. I wear your cross."

It was my turn. I stepped forward, the lay leader whispered, "The body of Christ," and I pinched off a piece of bread. Sam grabbed at it, and when I popped it in my mouth, he grasped my chin with both hands, feeling it move as I chewed. Why hadn't Todd and I traded off so we could do this in peace?

"The blood of Christ," said Father Joe as he handed me the cup. As Sam tried to grab it from me, I heard a few giggles from the pews. I quickly put it to my lips and gave it back. I hadn't even sipped, too afraid that Sam would dunk in his whole hand or bump it, spilling it all over me.

I hurried down the aisle, holding back tears. I couldn't even do communion right. Sam tried to shimmy free, but we had ten minutes or so before I could set him loose. As soon as I pulled him onto my lap, he started crying and going limp, then wriggling out of my hold. I had to get out of there. I picked him up onto my hip and marched us to the back.

God, I'm trying. But Sundays at home are looking better all the time. Did God even hear me?

I knew we weren't supposed to test God, to ask for a sign, but how I wanted one. It didn't have to be anything dramatic, just a little nod of sorts, saying "I see you reaching for me. I'm still here." Of course God could give me more than that. He could whisper in my ear something comforting, something like, "I know that being treated as a child is hard for you without work to comfort you. Let me show you the kind of child I want you to be."

If only God would! He could show me how to serve him in this new life of mine, or explain why on earth he kept luring me away from church—or was that God's doing at all? Was this just a big fat rationalization for my lazy, inattentive mind? Sam's wails grew louder. I'd have to take him out.

I pushed open the door and stepped out into the darkening sky, pulling my coat around me. If God wouldn't give me a sign, maybe I could give him one: the sign of the cross. Could I do it, to show him that I was his? It wouldn't make any difference, but I did want to do it, to drape his cross across me, to try it on, to show God that I meant it. No one else would see.

I looked up at the apartment balconies, up and down the street. No one was there. I brought my hand up and then put it down again, suddenly shy.

An old woman walked by, eyeing me over the fence. I watched her until she disappeared.

It was just Sam and me, so I had a debate with myself:

You're Baptist, not Catholic.

It's just a hand movement.

It's more than that.

Sam wiggled in my arms, so I set him down to toddle around in the grass. I waited until he was absorbed in catching a leaf as it skittered across the roots of a tree.

Go ahead.

I bowed my head just a little and touched my thumb and two fingers to my forehead, as if I had a headache.

Go on.

I touched my stomach, then, just slightly, touched to the right. Anyone would think I was straightening the collar of my coat. This was silly. I was ready to forget the whole thing, when my hand crossed over to touch my left shoulder, as if it had a mind of its own. Was it God, helping me talk to him? Or was it me, so intent on showing God that I wanted to be his child that my own body took over and finished the job?

"My Baptist wife," Todd would have teased, "the Catholic wannabe." He was always teasing me about how enamored I'd become by the saint cards, the crosses, and the Mary shrines around town—not to mention the cathedral and all its statues and paintings. Maybe Catholic France was soaking into my skin a little, but the cross felt right to me, a secret signal showing God I wanted to be his. Draping myself with an invisible cross was a symbol I'd keep just for me and God. No one else had to know.

I'd give it a holy card of its own. My hand raised before my torso, the tracing of a cross visible across me.

The tagline?

I am yours.

The prayer?

Dear God, with my whole mind, my whole body, my whole spirit, I want to show you how much I love you. There is so much I don't understand, but I do know that I belong to you. As I draw your cross across myself, bless me with knowledge of how to be your child, right where I am.

An autumn wind ruffled my skirt around my legs. Sam bent down to finger a pebble, and I could hear the pump organ start up inside, marking the last hymn of the service. It was finally almost time to go home, back to my easy life and my Madame Pink Suit dreams, all the while draped with the invisible Catholic cross.

Maybe I was a Catholic wannabe, but I'd bet they wouldn't mind me borrowing their cross for a while. Like the foreigner Ruth in a strange new land, I could follow after them, gleaning the fields of what they left behind.

Chapter 14
God in a Red Nose

The French don't do Halloween. They're too busy packing their suitcases and getting on trains, heading back to the family home for La Toussaint. All Saints Day is a national holiday in France, a time for good sons and daughters to lay wreathes on the graves of their departed loved ones, and a chance to honor the lesser known saints, the ones that aren't remembered on the calendar year. But for my kids, La Toussaint meant a week and a half of freedom from school and a long weekend in Paris.

Paris! The most beautiful city in the world!

Or so everyone said. I'd only seen the Charles de Gaulle airport, so I had no idea.

"Clermont is nothing," said my friend Virginie, "nothing compared to Paris."

Was it true? Clermont was stunning enough with its medieval fountains and cobblestone streets. "Everyone goes to Paris," I'd told my mother, as if I needed an excuse.

"Honey, you don't have to convince me. You can't live in France without going to Paris! Why are you hesitating?"

Why was I hesitating? Because my life was already a big vacation? That while my friends back home were running from work to dance to soccer to scouts, I was lolling around a café, planning my next vacation. A vacation from what? Coffee and shopping?

We took the late afternoon train and within fifteen minutes of boarding, I was sure we should have opted for the privacy of our own automobile and zipped up the autoroute while the kids slept. Instead, I kept constant watch on the door to our compartment, crossing my fingers that no one would slide it open and settle into the three empty seats. Unlike French children who spend their lives taking the train back and forth to *grand-mère's* house, our American kids were beside themselves, hoisting their backpacks on and off the overhead bins, opening and closing the pleated curtains, flipping the ashtray cover open and shut, and making several trips to the bathroom and the snack bar at the end of the train.

After an hour and a half, the novelty had worn thin. The kids had slipped into their usual routine of trying to irritate each other. Sarah had her nose in a book, but withdrew it periodically to complain about Ben's whistling. Ben answered her by whistling louder, cheering as he played his Game Boy. Sam, desperately in need of sleep, stormed around the tiny alley of floor space, whining and pulling things onto the floor. He'd crawl up onto a seat, lay his head down, and then jerk it up again, bleary eyed, fighting off sleep. Todd had just picked him up and was rocking him when I noticed a child staring at us through the glass doors.

She was about four or five years old and wore a plain purple sweater and knit pants. Her brown tangles reached her shoulders, and I shuddered to see that her face had been severely burned. Her right side had suffered more than her left, leaving one eye pulled lower than the other and the corner of her mouth frozen in a fixed position. She tilted her head and stared at Sam, pushed her nose against the glass of our window, and then reached for the door. Was she coming in?

"*Bonjour á tous,*" she said in a coarse little voice, sliding the door open.

I watched Ben and Sarah freeze in their seats. The little girl smiled her half smile at them, slid Sarah's books aside, and sat down beside her.

Sam wriggled to see who had come in and began to shriek at the sight of her. He hid his face in Todd's neck, but she was too busy fiddling with the red foam ball to notice. She started humming a circus tune, squeezed the ball, and fit it over her nose.

"There we go! Hello, little baby. Guess what? I'm a clown! My name is Clotilde." She grinned at Sam her half grin.

Sam peeked at her and wailed louder, turning away.

I wasn't sure what to do.

"Oh, don't cry," she said, putting her hands on her hips. "I heard you crying in here, and I've come in to make you laugh. Are you ready?" The little clown patted Sam's leg. "Which toy would you like?" she asked, emptying her pockets onto the seat beside her. "Would you like a ball, or a dinosaur, or maybe this elephant?" She made the blue elephant dance through the air towards Sam's face.

His scream turned to a pulsing cry.

"Sam, look what she has for you," Todd said, trying to smile at the little girl, and comfort Sam. "Look, a blue elephant." Sam screamed and clung to Todd.

"Sam, it's alright, honey," I said, smiling at Clotilde. "She just wants you to play,"

Sam sobbed loudly.

"Samuel is tired," I stammered in French. "Thank you, but he needs a nap." Ben and Sarah were still frozen on their seats, eyes wide.

Our little clown would not give up.

"Maybe a ball then," she said, touching Sam's hand with the ball. "Cou cou!" she called, bouncing the ball down his arm. Sam pulled his hand away and buried his face in Todd's shoulder.

"Do you like dinosaurs? Everybody likes dinosaurs."

"Merci, " I said, touching her shoulder, "but I think he is too tired to play."

She tilted her head and looked at me. "All right then," she said, and gathered her toys back into her pockets. "Au revoir, Samuel!" Clotilde slipped out of our compartment, still wearing the red nose.

For the next half hour, as the train rumbled through the suburbs of Paris and into the city, the children couldn't stop talking about Clotilde.

"She was so nice," Sarah said.

"We should find her and say thank you," Ben said.

But she was gone.

As we wandered around the Metro, searching for the train to the hotel, I tried to shepherd Ben and Sarah up and down the steps and take it all in. A band of Rastafarians played flutes and drums in one tunnel, and in another, a man with a beard played "Hava Nagila" on the accordion.

We finally made it to our stop, and I had just paused for a moment to figure out what a poster of a naked man wearing high heels was advertising when an Audrey Hepburn look-alike almost pierced my right clog with the heel of her stilettos.

The city streets glowed in the lamplight as we walked in a line with our suitcases. Todd was first with the stroller and I brought up the rear, making sure we didn't lose anyone. Ben and Sarah were all eyes, watching the crowds spilling out of restaurants, the couples arm in arm strolling down the street, the taxis and buses whizzing by, and a man sitting on the sidewalk in the dark, playing a guitar.

"Paris sure is different from Clermont," Ben said, looking back at him.

"Yeah," said Sarah. "It's pretty and a little scary all at the same time. Mama, do you think we'll see Clotilde again?"

"I doubt it," I said. "This is a really big city. But you never know."

Ben nodded, but I noticed him scanning the people, looking for her.

The next morning Clotilde was still on their minds. "Come on," Sarah said, pulling me toward the carousel on the Champs de Mars, near the Eiffel Tower. "Can we go? Clotilde might be there. Please?"

"OK. But I wouldn't count on seeing Clotilde again. Remember what I said about how big Paris is?"

A young twenty-something was lugging painted horses out of a shed and hooking them onto the hand-cranked carousel. He wasn't in the least bit of a hurry, carrying a horse in one hand and snacking on a baguette with Nutella in the other.

"Wouldn't want to rush things," Todd grumbled to himself as he pulled the stroller over to a bench and sat down.

Todd was still a little cranky. Unlike the rest of us, he was not feeling so entranced by Paris. We'd been up since six in the morning, and when we had tromped down the hotel stairs at seven o'clock for the breakfast we had paid for, no one was anywhere to be found. It had taken us forty-five minutes to find an open café. My husband needed his coffee.

Strangely enough, the same thing had happened at the Eiffel Tower. We were first in line there at nine, but at 9:40, ten minutes past the posted opening time, the ticket box was still closed.

"I don't get it," he grumbled to the Chinese tourists behind us. "Parisians have no respect for time at all."

It didn't make sense. Hadn't Madame Mallet gone on and on about how hectic life is in Paris, how uncivilized they are, so controlled by the clock?

Finally the carousel man gave a nod to my children, and they ran through the gate to find their horses. Ben chose the horse labeled Bijou and tied the worn belt around his waist. Sarah took Sam by the hand and buckled them both into a buggy. Two little French girls in dresses hopped on, and the man handed out batons. "What is this for?" Ben asked. When we shrugged our shoulders, the man called out "It's a baton. For this," and he waved it around like a jousting lance, spearing it through a brass ring.

He turned the crank, and around they went, with no music, except for the birds and the laughter of the children from the playground.

A little girl with brown hair and a purple jumper ran up from behind me and stood by the low fence, watching the carousel turn. No, it wasn't Clotilde. I fingered the miniature Eiffel Tower souvenir on my lap and remembered her dancing the elephant through the air.

For the rest of the day she tagged along in my thoughts, all through the streets of Paris and back to the hotel as we returned for a nap.

Todd approached the lady at the desk. "I have a question, please."

"Yes, monsieur?"

"Did we misunderstand each other last night when I checked in? My family came down for breakfast this morning, but no one was here."

"What time did you come?"

"At seven o'clock. We waited until half past seven, but no one came."

"No, monsieur. We were here at seven."

"I don't think so, madame. I was here, and I looked at my watch."

The woman squinted at Todd and pursed her lips in thought. Suddenly a hint of a smile turned up the corner of her mouth.

"You were aware of the time change, sir?"

"The time change . . ?"

"Yes, sir. The time changes every fall. *Heure d'hiver.*

Todd closed his eyes and laughed.

The lady nervously began to explain how the time change works, and why we have a time change and when in the calendar history they began having time changes.

"Yes, I know," Todd said. "I understand now. Thank you."

"I can't believe it," he said as we walked up to our room. "I completely forgot about the time change."

"You'd think they'd publicize that," I said, trying to make him feel better, "at least for the tourists."

"We're not children," Todd said. "We should have thought of that ourselves."

It was true, but we acted like kids for the rest of the day, eating crêpes sugared with Nutella and bananas for lunch, passing by museums to let the kids ride the pedal cars in the park and watch the street performers entertain the crowd at the Jardin des Tuileries. We'll be in France for years, I thought, as we stopped to watch a clown standing as still as a statue on a box. There'll be plenty of time for museums.

"Can I give him some money? Please, please, please?" Ben begged.

Todd pulled a ten-franc from his pocket, and Ben walked shyly up to the clown and dropped it in his hat. A crowd began to gather as the clown came to life, doing a little wind-up dance. Everyone clapped as he handed Ben a tissue paper flower and then pressed his own red nose, turning himself back into a statue again. The red nose . . . Clotilde . . . our sweet little jester.

"For Christ's sake we are fools," Paul wrote of the apostles of Jesus. I'd always loved that image: Christ's followers as a tattered band of fools; clowns, clothed in rags, following the ways of God, foolish to the world. My little train jester was a carefree fool like that, a stunning, generous fool.

We had played our way through Paris like Clotilde, freeing ourselves from all control as we ate and drank and strolled through the parks. It was too beautiful to rush. The tourists could stick to their schedules, but I wanted to savor every fountain, every street musician, every cup of café au lait. Home was just a few hours away. We could always come back for more.

Thank you, God, for all of this, especially for Clotilde, I muttered to myself. Thank you for helping me let go of control, even if I didn't mean to.

As we strolled along the Jardin des Tuileries in the autumn chill, I found myself scanning the crowd for Clotilde. As if God would bring her to me, I laughed to myself, and then I stopped short. Why, God had done it already. Hadn't I wished back at church that God would show me the kind of child he wanted me to be? And then, one week later, Clotilde slides open the door and walks into my life. France might be making me into a child again, helpless and dependent, but she was the child I wanted to be, one who had her own wounds yet didn't hide away, who trusted the world to love her anyway, never thinking for a moment she might be unwelcome.

Saint Clotilde needed a card of her own. But I didn't want to draw her half smile or the burns of her face; I wanted to focus on the effect she had on us, to show the light inside her, the hope and kindness and generosity she pulled out of her pockets to share with us. I could see it now.

We'd pose in front of the Tour Eiffel, all wearing red foam clown noses: Todd with his watch, still not fallen forward in time; me in my clogs, guidebook in hand; Sarah with her book and the baton from the carousel; Ben with his Game Boy in one hand and a tissue paper flower in the other; and Sam with the blue elephant, flying it through the air.

It'd make a great tagline:

Fools for God

And the prayer?

> Dear God, make us saints who won't give up, quick to jump into a compartment of strangers and hand out blessings and make babies smile. Make us fools for your sake, God, unafraid and unhurried by the clock, confident that there is enough love to go around and that we can always come back for more.

As we walked along with the masses, I felt such joy inside me, fizzing like the cider! Joy and relief! So what if God was playing peekaboo with me at church—or whenever I tried to force seeking him in any way. I didn't need to worry. Of course God loved me. Of course I was not alone.

I looked at the sky and suddenly wished I could spin myself up into it, just to see how we looked from the clouds, far above the words and wounds that separate us, to see my family flowing in a holy sea of people, rolling past the rows of trees lined up on the bank as if to watch, their leaves turning yellow and orange and brown.

Chapter 15

Saint Béchamel

On our first Thanksgiving Day in France, the children went off to school and Todd left for work as if it were any other Thursday, which in France of course it was. I mentioned Thanksgiving to Madame Mallet, and she asked me if it had anything to do with Buffalo Bill. I tried to explain but finally gave up and went inside. I wished I could call Mother, but it was two in the morning in North Carolina, and she wouldn't be up to put the turkey in the oven for a few more hours.

I'd told Mother all about the turkey problem: that though a family-sized *rôti de dinde* was beautifully presented at the *boucherie*, wrapped with a belt of pork fat and neatly tied with string, a single rôti could have fed at most maybe one of my uncles. "You can order a whole turkey at *Boeuf à Gogo*," I'd said, "but you have to bring a cage, and I just wasn't willing."

Mother thought this was funny and went on and on about how glad she was that the kids would still get to celebrate the holiday even though we couldn't be with family. I didn't tell her that though I was happy for the turkey and the pumpkin pie, I found it a bummer that we'd have to sit through church to get it.

Sorry, God, I prayed, but did we really have to go to church to celebrate Thanksgiving? Of course it made sense to do it—who were we thanking anyway?—but church was never part of the deal back home. God, yes. Church, no. Thanksgiving meant a five-hour drive to Mom and Dad's or to my in-laws' house, a heartfelt prayer, and a nice meal. Did we really have to go to church to express our thanks? Couldn't we say thank you to God in the privacy of our own homes, over our own platter of twin rôtis de dinde?

"But the meal's a good fundraiser for the church," Todd said. "It draws lots of people who don't normally go to church. And they bring their French friends too. Don't you want to share Thanksgiving with your friends?"

But if you have to entice people to church by dangling a turkey in front of their noses, was it really worth it? Would the service be that meaningful to people who only came for pumpkin pie? Couldn't we just combine the church with the meal? Make it sort of a Christian dinner theater?

Todd asked me what was bugging me, and I mumbled some excuse. I just didn't want to be reminded in front of a whole new crop of people that although God sent me messages through little girls and crazy old men, women on motorbikes and prostitutes, I didn't seem to get on well at church. Christ Church was one of the first homemade saint cards of my heart, the chapel I'd hoped to center my faith, but every time I got there it seemed God had stepped out for a coffee.

Yes, I'd go with everyone else to church, but I'd make my own Thanksgiving dinner on the actual holiday, in spite of the catered feast to come.

The meal turned out fairly well if I do say so myself. I cooked two rôtis and made a sweet potato soufflé, garlic green beans, and stuffing from baguettes. I even bought a pumpkin at Marché St. Pierre and made a pie from scratch. After it was over, Todd and I lingered at the table over coffee.

"Great dinner, Beck," he said. "It's got my taste buds all primed for Sunday, when Monsieur Desnoyer steps up to bat."

"Oh really?" I said, picturing me picking up a bat of my own with which to wallop my husband for being so clueless. I let him talk. Maybe I wanted a fight.

"I'm glad I told Art I'd help him get the Thanksgiving meal organized, or else I wouldn't have gotten to know Monsieur Desnoyer. Just wait 'til you meet him. He runs this smoky little brasserie behind the tire factory—I'll have to take you there sometime. You know how those places always make things like *croque monsieurs* and *steak-frites*?

I nodded.

"Well, he whips up *porc au Camembert*—whatever he wants. And his kitchen's no bigger than ours!"

"Uh huh."

"I asked him how he got started, and he said he was made to be happy in the kitchen, that he had to do it or he'd drive his wife crazy cooking at home. He's got a real passion for it. He still has this Thanksgiving wreath on his wall that the ladies gave him the first year he started doing it. I think that was two or three years ago."

"Good for him," I said. "You know, you might not want to go on and on about somebody else's cooking with someone who's just spent her whole day in the kitchen fixing your meal."

"Oh," Todd said. "I wasn't thinking. Sorry. It was an amazing meal, Beck."

"It's OK," I said. Suddenly I didn't feel like fighting.

Monsieur Desnoyer was made to be happy in the kitchen, and the man in Ambert was made to sing. What was I made for?

Nothing had changed by Sunday. The minute we walked in the chapel, Sam turned into a whirlwind, popping up and sitting down, pulling on my shirt, storming around, knocking over whatever was in his path. We spent most of the service in the back running around the Flames of Hell. Unfortunately I was concentrating so much on keeping the toddler away from the heater that within two minutes he had eaten an old Cheerio he found under the pew and stabbed his leg with a pencil.

By the time lunch came around, Sam was exhausted. The children's school let the church host the meal in its cafeteria, so Todd pushed Sam in the stroller around the tables as everyone arrived, hoping he would settle down as I got Ben and Sarah situated at the children's table. Where would Todd and I sit? Jessie and Cindy had already found seats.

"You can sit with us if you like," said Natalie. She was nice and spoke French like a native. She had also apparently adopted the French notion that the female breast was just another appendage, more beautiful than an arm or leg, but nothing to blush about. As I took my seat, she pulled her newborn out of the baby seat and onto her lap and began unbuttoning her shirt. The men at the other end of the table were so busy talking business that no one seemed to notice.

"So, Becky," she said, working her way down to her belly button, "now that you've been here a while and are all settled, have you decided what you're going to do with all your time in France?"

"I kind of have my hands busy with Sam," I said.

"Oh I know that," she said, fishing a burp cloth out of her bag. "Being mommy is a full-time job. But everybody makes time for fun. What do you like to do when you're not with the kids?"

"Well, I . . . uh . . ."

"What did you do before you moved here?" she asked, pulling her shirt to one side, exposing half of her lacy bra. I glanced up at Todd, who was walking up behind her, unaware. He bent down to hand Sam off to me, and slipped into a seat across from Natalie at the exact moment she pulled down the flap of her nursing bra, exposing her lily white breast for all to see. Surprised, Todd spun around in his chair, stood up again, and walked over to the wine table to get in line to buy a bottle.

Good thing. I could use a glass or two.

Natalie didn't notice, being too busy positioning her newborn for maximum suction.

"I used to do a lot of stuff. All the free time has been a real adjustment here."

"Really? Like what?"

I started to rattle off a list of activities: my volunteer tutoring, the church committees, my help at Cottonwood Elementary.

"No. I mean fun. You know, going to a book club or to classes at a gym—stuff like that."

I nodded. "Yes, I was in a club for a while." I left out the details. My neighbor Marsha had twisted my arm into joining a Bunco club with some other neighbors, but I quit after two meetings. I felt silly now to admit it, but I had thought it was a waste of time, getting together with no other purpose than to eat and drink and play dice. Now I felt sorry for my old workaholic self.

Finally Natalie put her breasts away, Art stood at the front to welcome everyone, and Todd returned with the wine.

"Get an eyeful there?" I whispered.

He nodded.

"So where's your Mr. Magic? Monsieur Desnoyer? Shouldn't he be here by now?"

"I know," Todd said, giving the door a worried glance. "Art says he comes in at the very last minute so that the food is at the perfect temperature."

He was certainly cutting it close. We finished the sixth verse of "Over the River and Through the Woods," but Monsieur Desnoyer was nowhere to be seen.

No one else seemed concerned. Sam was grabbing all of my silverware and Father Joe was performing a terribly long reading of George Washington's Thanksgiving Proclamation, when suddenly the side cafeteria double doors swung wide open. A gust of wind scattered leaves into the room as a driver backed an old van up to the doorway. Everyone's eyes turned to the chef.

Monsieur Desnoyer quickly inspected the buffet tables as Father Joe continued reading. He was just as Todd had described: a sturdy man with wooly eyebrows and a neat mustache. He nodded to his assistant, who opened the van doors wide, and suddenly more assistants appeared, pulling out stainless steel pans of steaming food and arranging them on the tables with carefully orchestrated precision, as if the choreography was part of the show.

Dinner was magnificent. Monsieur Desnoyer stood behind the buffet with his assistants, ladling food onto our plates. When I handed him my plate and asked for just a little bit of stuffing, he clicked his tongue and looked in my eyes and said, "So little for you? *Ah, non. Prenez plus, madame.*" Take more. I was glad I did.

The turkey was perfectly moist, stuffed with chestnuts and morels, more flavorful than any turkey I'd ever tasted in a lifetime of Thanksgivings. The béchamel sauce on the cauliflower almost brought tears to my eyes. Todd and I took turns eating and bouncing Sam on our laps until Sarah was finished and took over.

I asked Natalie how the chef knew how to fix the American dishes. "A committee picked out the recipes," she said. "And then we translated them into French, and made the metric conversions, and added little notes such as 'should be a little salty,' and 'springs back to the touch.' And he took some license to make the dishes his own, which was good, I think."

Good? It was glorious! God certainly had created him for the kitchen. As Sam finally fell asleep in his stroller, I watched Monsieur Desnoyer set out the cheese plates. He stood behind them, smiling occasionally, saying, "Prenez plus, monsieur." Take more.

As I watched him standing before us, radiating love like God in an apron, Monsieur Desnoyer became my newest saint: Saint Béchamel, father of the father sauces, smooth and warm and delightful to the taste, calling forth the deliciousness of whatever it touches. I'd draw him as he was, with his wooly eyebrows and quick feet, dancing in at exactly the right moment, supplying everything the soul hungers for, both nourishment and delight.

The perfect tagline came straight from his mouth:

Take more.

And the prayer?

Dear God, you set before us a feast of blessings and call us to the table. Forgive us when we want to take over the cooking ourselves. Help us fill our plates and come back for more.

As we drove home, sleepy and full, a cold rain began to fall. The scenery passed by, blurred by the raindrops on my window: the houses webbed with ivy, the purple red leaves beginning to fall, a woman with an umbrella walking her dog. "*Prenez plus, Madame.*" Take, eat, Madame Pink Suit had said, and now God was repeating it. "Take more, madame; take more." Take more of this beautiful life I'm giving you, even as I play hide-and-seek with you, even as I love you through this funk you're in.

A surge of thankfulness swept through me, gratitude for the chance to try on this life, for a cafeteria full of friends, for the taste of morels, for the sound of my children talking to each other, for my husband's warm hand, and for Baby Sam's sweet pink lips rising and falling as he slept in his car seat.

Yes, God. I will take more.

Chapter 16
An Arm and a Leg for God

It might be December, but France was as beautiful as ever. It wasn't a summer kind of loveliness she had, rosy cheeked with flowers in her hair, but more a raw, naked kind of beauty. With no shaggy ivy climbing up the houses or roses tumbling down the walls, I could see the elegance of the skeleton underneath, the rippling rooftops, the bare birches against the gray sky.

I poured myself another cup of coffee and went to see what everyone else was doing on this lazy Sunday morning. With the shutters closed, the living room was a dark, cozy cave. Todd sat at the computer, Ben was setting up green army guys all over the dining room table, Sam was playing at Todd's feet, and Sarah was lying on the couch with a book. We'd had our fun outside the day before, going on a blustery hike through the vineyards on the hill above the village. Today everyone was happy to stay in pajamas as our fairy godmother ticked the time slowly by.

"Thanks, honey," Todd said as I handed him a second cup of coffee. "I've got something for you too." He fished an envelope from a pile on the corner desk. "I was going to surprise you with this on Christmas," he said, handing it to me, "but I think you might like an early surprise."

As I opened it, he couldn't wait to explain. "See? It's tickets to a gospel concert, right before New Year's," he said. "Christophe was talking about it at work and asked if we'd like to go with him and Amelie. What do you think?"

"Are you kidding? Of course I want to go!" A gospel concert was exactly what I needed, music throbbing with God's spirit, unmeasured, uncontrolled, wild. Not only that, but this would give us a chance to introduce something uniquely American to French friends! After six months on the receiving end of all sorts of French treasures, it would feel nice to do the sharing for a change.

"Great," Todd said. "I thought we'd take the kids—Christophe said they're bringing Marthe. It should be something to see."

I nodded. I just couldn't imagine the French, who show such little emotion in public, clapping and swaying with the music and shouting an occasional amen.

"Look, I've got the kids," Todd said. "Why don't you call some friends and head to the flea market? Go enjoy yourself. We'll have plenty of together time at church tonight."

Maybe I'd do just that: follow the direction of my husband and Saint Béchamel and take more.

Cindy was busy doing chores for their move, so it was just Jessie and me. We'd barely walked the aisles two minutes when she started her typical flea market behavior—weaving back and forth, getting engrossed in long conversations with the vendors, waving me to go on ahead.

I didn't mind. As I walked by the tables, I recognized most of the faces behind them. The weasel man called out, "Hello American girl," and I nodded at him and smiled. I passed the linen lady with a friendly wave and the poster guy who had hiked his foot on the table and showed me his American boots when I told him where I was from. This was my new congregation; these were my compatriots. As I started down the next aisle, the clouds parted and the sun poured through, warming my face. I watched everyone squinting in the bright light. God was lavishing it on everyone. We were all beautiful nobodies, loved by God the same.

I'd nearly made it to the end of the second aisle when I noticed a vendor I'd never seen before. She was in her fifties, wearing a red coat, her gray hair in bouncy curls charging from beneath her black beret. She wore white gloves, not the poufy kind to keep her hands warm, but thin white ones, as if she were going to do a magic trick. Or maybe she was handling something special and didn't want to dirty it with the oils from her skin. She had just begun to unpack her trunk, displaying various silver items on a large square of black velvet. They glinted in the light. What were they? A trio of men leaned over the table, blocking my sight. I squeezed through the crowd to take a closer look.

How strange. They were miniature body parts, crafted in silver, like Christmas tree ornaments, none more than five inches wide. Who would put a liver on a tree? There was a leg from upper thigh to foot; an open hand, palm up; a flaming heart adorned with filigree; and a belly, complete with a belly button and engraved with the letters VF (*ventre fronte?* front stomach?). The silver pieces were mostly flat, except for the belly that was rounded a bit, finely crafted and detailed, as if they'd come straight out of *Gray's Anatomy*.

The men huddled over them, examining them like doctors prepped for surgery. They seemed particularly interested in the set of eyes, complete with eyebrows and the bridge of a nose. What would they do with something like that? Christmas was three weeks away, but who would ask Père Nöel for a tin foot?

The vendor stopped to search the back of her van, pulling out boxes and putting them back again. Finally she wiggled another box out of the bottom of the stack, opened it on the table, and began adding silver animals to the body parts: a donkey, a goat, and a rabbit. The men ahhed in appreciation, and immediately huddled in for a better look.

I didn't want to interrupt. Jessie might know what they were.

I found her an aisle away, chatting with a twenty-something man in a top hat who held an old book of racy postcards. By the time I dragged her back to the velvet-topped table, the men had gone. Had they bought up the lot? No, only the pair of eyes and maybe a couple of animals seemed to be missing.

Jessie examined each one, turning them in her hand as I tried to catch the lady's attention. "I think they're ex votos—you know, prayer ornaments," Jessie said. "Like Mexican Milagros. Have you seen those?"

I shook my head.

"You find them in churches all over. You should see the ones in Marseilles. There are tons of them in the cathedral there—mostly paintings of boats and three-dimensional models that fishermen have brought in over the years. They leave them in the church, hoping it will help God remember them."

The vendor confirmed it.

"Parishioners used to pin them on the shrines of the saints in church, to remind them of their prayer request. Let's say you have an ailment in your leg," she said, lifting up her leg to be sure I understood. "You might buy the leg ornament and pin it to the shrine of a saint. Or the leg could even be symbolic, to ask for a blessing for an upcoming journey—to England, for example," she said, offering us a smile.

How kind for her to acknowledge that she thought we were British! As Jessie moved on to the next table, I thanked the lady and shook her hand.

"You like the heart, don't you," she said to me.

"Yes, it's beautiful." It was beautiful, a valentine heart as big as the palm of my hand, with flames streaming from the top.

"You might need it for yourself?"

I nodded.

She nodded back. "Are you blessed with love?" she asked. "Or heartache?"

"Oh I'm blessed, very blessed with love," I said. "But maybe there's a small ache there, a very small one. A puzzle, I think, maybe not a pain." Now that I said it, I think I believed it. My strange situation with God and church was a puzzle, not so much a pain.

"Heartache can be a blessing too."

"Yes?"

"Oh yes. Without it, one might never move on. Find the next adventure. Live the life one is meant to have. Yes?"

"Yes." How I loved having an existential conversation over a table at the flea market with a stranger. How I loved France.

"I saw you liked that sacred heart. Why didn't you buy it?" Jessie asked as we walked back to the car.

"The sacred heart?"

"Yeah, you know. That's what they call it: *sacré cœur*. I'm sure you've seen it in paintings and on Jesus statues, the heart with the flames coming out. Most of the time it has a cross in the flames and it might be wrapped in thorns. It comes from this nun back in the seventeenth century who saw visions of Jesus in which he showed her his heart. It's supposed to remind us of Christ's love for humankind, no matter what. Blah, blah, blah. So why didn't you get one?"

I shrugged my shoulders.

Of course God didn't need a metal trinket to remember my calls for his help. Knock and the door shall be opened, right? I'd been knocking my whole life and God's presence had always been there, whether I was being judge-y or not. It must be there still. God might lead me in a different direction, maybe into my next adventure, like the lady at the market said, but he wouldn't leave me. If God was leading and I was meant to follow, where was God going?

Later that evening as I stood in line at church for the bread and wine, feeling as spiritual as a brick, I wasn't so sure. My prayers were settling on the floor like the morning's fog, kicked around by our feet. As I shivered in my coat, I wasn't exactly disappointed anymore; my hope was locked up safe within my own silver heart.

But if I had bought that heart, I would have just slipped it under the altar cloth when no one was looking. It couldn't hurt anything. It would remind God that I was trying to reach him. I wasn't giving up on church yet, no matter how much it felt like a waste—could I say that?—a waste of time.

When my turn with the chalice finally came, I took a big gulp of the wine. Please God, slip down my throat and all the way to my legs, like holy cement. Keep them from walking me out the door.

Todd handed Sam off to me to take his turn at the table, and I concentrated on feeling Sam's weight on my lap as he shifted from side to side, grounding me. But within a few seconds he stopped being helpful. I might have been fidgety, but my toddler son was a holy roller, clapping his hands and babbling along with a hymn that played in his head, whether we were singing or not.

"No, no, Sammy," I whispered in his ear and tried to ply him with toys.

Art whispered in my ear from the pew behind me, "It looks like you've got a Baptist preacher on your hands."

I nodded and pretended that I thought it was funny and pressed a cracker into Sam's hand. He pushed the entire thing in his mouth, holding it closed with a finger.

After he finally swallowed it, he pulled on my chin and said, "Moe." I didn't have any more.

"Here," I whispered, getting a crayon and notepad out of my bag. "Sammy draw?"

Sam shook his head, stood up again and started babbling again. The entire congregation turned to look and shuffled us out of the pew. We'd finish the service outside—again.

The street lamp cast a circle of light on the church lawn. We stepped into it and looked back at the chapel. It was a wonder, so beautifully old and quaint. I remembered how excited I'd been when I first saw it, assuming we'd acclimate quickly in such a small church. Many of our fellow churchgoers had talked about how they had never been very active in their churches back in the States, but church was my second home. Yet I felt so out of place.

Sam was all hands, trying to touch the pebbles underneath a bush, the sprigs of grass, and an occasional twig or dry leaf, and I followed behind, taking everything out of his fist before he could put it in his mouth. Finally he got bored and crawled up the steps, brushing aside my steadying hand. He reached for the door handle and patted the door. "Moe," he said.

"More church?" I asked.

He smiled and pulled on the handle again.

"No, Sammy." I didn't want more.

A moped buzzed down the street. It was a teenage boy dressed in black, not Madame Pink Suit, no pretty legs, no scarf billowing. There was no one to rescue me. I had the urge to buzz away from here, buckle Sammy in a seat behind me and take off for home. At least if I had taken the car keys, Sam could've climbed over everything without bothering anyone. We still had the Lord's Prayer, another hymn, and Sunday School to get through. This would take forever.

This morning at the flea market I'd felt positively bathed in his peace. My heart had felt so full that it almost ached. Too bad that in church it was metal, hollow, and flat.

I sat Sammy on the steps beside me and followed my fingers after his, ruffling the lichen on the stone. I imagined myself walking back up the aisle, laying my heart on the altar cloth for the Holy Spirit to fill again.

Even though I didn't buy it, that silver valentine heart with the scalloped edges and sprouting flames could be mine forever on my newest holy card. Beams of divine light would radiate from it, just as they did from Jesus' chest in paintings and on statues, reminding me of Christ's love for humanity (that's me!) no matter what.

The tagline would read:

Fill her up, Lord.

It sounded a little crass, but it's exactly what I wanted to say. And the prayer?

Sacré Cœur, who loves us wholeheartedly, no matter what, we praise you for being with us wherever we are, whether we're clapping along to your song or running out the door. Thank you for blessing us with your deep and abiding love, love that helps us raise our heads to find you in the midst of the heartaches life sometimes doles out to us. Empty our hearts of ourselves enough to make more room for you.

Church let out, but I was still praying: Please fill my heart for Christmas, God. It's all I want this year.

Chapter 17
The Church Comes with Handcuffs

On the last school day before *les vacances de Noël*, the aisles of Auchan were finally packed with holiday shoppers. I'd asked Virginie a few weeks earlier where the frenzied crowds were, and she'd said, "It's a Christian celebration, not the January sales. The waiting makes Christmas more special."

It also makes it crazy. Mothers and fathers were madly storming the aisles, loading up their carts with toys for *les enfants*, wrapping paper, and boxes of *chocolat*, while I, on the other hand, stood in a forgotten corner, hoping that no one would see me and discover my embarrassing secret.

When I asked a clerk for help, he sensed my humiliation and led me like a child through the crowds to the correct aisle. "Here we are, madame," he said, and handed me the biggest mousetrap I'd ever seen. I shivered at the picture printed on the wooden slat. It was the tough city rat of my nightmares. His tail curled up above his head, under-lining his name, <u>Lucifer</u>.

How I detest mice.

Never in my adult life had a mouse or rat invaded my home, nibbling on our crumbs, wiping the floor with its reptilian tail, and leaving its mouse waste wherever it squatted. I still couldn't believe it: We had a mouse—in my sanctuary, the one place in France where I felt completely at ease, where I could talk freely without anyone staring, where I could let down my guard and not have to pretend that every-thing was great. The fortress of my house had been invaded, even if I'd only seen it in the garage. My perfect peace was spoiled. I had a mouse.

Could it have been my imagination . . . a ball of gray fluff, blowing across the floor of the garage as I gathered a load of whites into the washer? I'd spied movement out of the corner of my eye and wondered what had fallen out of a pants pocket. A ball of yarn . . . a yo-yo? But there had been no clatter—only silence as the gray mouse ambled across the cement floor, in no particular hurry.

I froze. As I swooped up the basket onto my hip, our cat Katie opened an eyelid from a nap and sat up to watch the mouse scurry around the corner. I ran on tiptoes back into the house, and as I shut the door, Katie darted inside. Some cat . . .

If there was one mouse, were there more? Were they inside my house, too? I walked through my house, scanning the floor from room to room for bits of paper or droppings. There were none that I could see.

I would not tell the children. They would share the excitement with their friends, and within an hour my house would be known in the expatriate community as The House with Mice. People would speculate about my cleanliness.

Todd would have to do something.

After the kids had gone to bed, I broke the news. He was not helpful.

"That explains a lot," he said. "Katie has been acting weird for the last couple of days. I didn't want to tell you, but I thought I heard scratching the other night in our room."

"In our room . . . Mice were in my bedroom? "What are you going to do? I'll go get you the phone book."

"Becky, it's nine-thirty at night. Everything closed two hours ago. I don't know what you want me to do, but whatever it is, you're going to have to wait until tomorrow."

"OK, but you'll have to do something first thing. I want that mouse gone by tomorrow night. I won't tolerate it in my house."

Todd narrowed his eyebrows. "Beck, you need to relax. I think you're overreacting."

"How am I supposed to relax? We have mice in our house!"

"So what? It's cold outside. Stray mice wander in. It happens to everybody. Just go to Auchan tomorrow and buy some traps. I'll come home for lunch and set them."

We had to have traps? "Isn't there another way, where I wouldn't have to see the mouse again?"

"What do you want?" Todd laughed. "Should I buy a flute?"

"It's not funny."

"OK, OK. You buy the traps, and I'll take care of it. You won't have to touch any dead mice."

So I went to bed, listening for each creak, each squeak of our bed, each rustle of the covers, trying not to imagine mice shimmying up our covers, dancing in my hair as I slept, brushing their little whiskers on my face.

And now I had Lucifer.

"See," the clerk said, "You put a little camembert here, and set it like this, and . . ." He drew his finger across his neck, and gave a little squeak.

"Do you have anything smaller?" I asked. "It's just a small mouse."

"Are you sure?" he asked. "Did you see it?"

"Oh, yes."

"No, we don't. But, madame I assure you, this will kill your mouse—no matter its size. And if it doesn't, perhaps you could get a cat."

"I have a cat. She's afraid of the mouse."

"It's an English cat?"

"No, American."

"American," the man laughed, "and it doesn't want to fight?"

Todd came home at lunch to set the trap for Lucifer, and for the rest of the afternoon I listened for the snap of the trap. It never came. Just to be sure, I snuck out to the garage on tiptoes every half hour, checking for any bloodied corpse.

There were none, not even by the next morning.

Thankfully we had Saturday plans away to get out of town for the day, to see the Romanesque basilica in the tiny village of Orcival. Someone at work had told Todd about its crèche, a nativity set in Provençal style—perfect for generating some Christmas spirit.

As we drove through Clermont and out again, into the green hills now yellowed and bare, I thought how strange this Christmas would be. My calendar was usually jam-packed with church activities and parties filling the weeks of Advent. Now the pages were mostly blank. We always packed up the kids and visited our parents the week after Christmas, but now it would just be the five of us. A quieter Christmas would be peaceful, as long as we could get rid of the mouse.

I looked at my watch. It was ten o'clock. Cindy's flight to Paris had left an hour ago, the first leg of her move back home. She'd be at Charles de Gaulle by now.

I was a little embarrassed that I'd thought we were so close. As I walked up with all the coffee ladies to the café on Friday, everyone jostled for a place beside her, trying to get in a few last thank-you's and good wishes. I followed behind, struggling with the stroller around the construction work on rue de Grande Bretagne.

It took three tables to seat us all. Even Patrick, the café owner, was sad to see Cindy go and sprung for mulled wine for everyone for a celebratory toast. From the far end of the table I watched her laugh between Ann and Missy, her friends who had arrived in France the same summer she had, three and a half years ago. I listened as they shared stories about Cindy that I'd never heard before. Of course I wasn't her closest friend. She had been taking care of me, just like she had for nearly everyone around the table when they were newcomers. I'd been one of many expats she'd nurtured.

The smoke in the café was thick, and Sam started squirming in his seat and fussing. It was time to go. I could say my last goodbyes later anyway since Cindy was coming over for lunch. I whispered my goodbyes to Jessie and Barbara and scooted out the door. Two steps onto the street, Missy came after me. "We're taking Cindy out to her favorite restaurant today for lunch. Do you want to come? We're meeting everybody at Le Soleil at one."

"Oh," I said. "No, sorry, but I've got Sam. He doesn't do too well in places like that. I'll have to say my goodbyes at school."

"Aw," Missy said. "That's too bad. We'll miss you."

"It's alright," I said, forcing a smile. "Have a good time."

My face felt hot. No, I refused to cry.

Todd turned on the radio and I leaned my head on the window, feeling the coldness of the glass. At least now we'd have a two-week break from racing the kids to school every morning and practicing *poesies* (poetry) and *dictées* (spelling) every night. As much as I loved the family gatherings at Christmas, it had to be more peaceful to stay home. Maybe the trap would even catch the mouse by the time we got home and I could stop thinking about it.

"Look!" Ben shouted from the backseat. "It's snowing!"

It was. Ben and Sarah started cheering. Even Sam got in the act, yelling and clapping in his car seat, with no idea what he was celebrating.

In minutes the pastures were frosted. "Do you think we should go back?" I asked, watching the sky fill with snow.

"The road's fine," Todd said. "See? It's melting on the pavement."

We followed the ribbon of black through the whitening woods. The tiny village of Orcival was tucked in a little valley down from the road, its twelfth-century Romanesque church the dominant feature of the village. With its rough gray exterior it looked like a stone version of a hermit crab, as if it had backed its way in and burrowed into the hillside. Chapels fanned out from the building in scallop shells, and the short octagonal steeple was topped with a spire.

Ben and Sarah were so excited about the snow. Already several inches blanketed the churchyard. I'd barely called out, "Zip those coats," before Ben and Sarah threw themselves down on a snowy bank, flapping their angel wings. I lifted Sam out of his seat and he toddled over to lie between them, blinking as snowflakes fell on his eyelashes.

Sarah pulled herself up. "I almost forgot! Madame Bioche said to look for the handcuffs on the church walls."

"Handcuffs on the walls? That's one way to keep people at church," I laughed to Todd.

"No, I'm serious," Sarah said, pulling us toward the front door.

We stood back, scanning the walls.

"They're supposed to be somewhere here on the outside," Sarah said.

We walked around the church, the snow blowing on our faces, and sure enough, there they were: several sets of shackles and balls with chains, mounted high above the doors.

"Who put them there?" Ben asked, shading his eyes from the glare of the sun on the snow. "How'd they get them up so high? What are they there for?"

"Whoa," Todd said, putting Sam into his baby backpack as I got out the guidebook, "one question at a time."

"Here it is," I said. "It says, 'Chains have been hung from the blind arcades in the southern part of the transept, next to the entrance, in thanksgiving for released prisoners.'"

Ben made a face. "They were keeping somebody in prison in church?"

"No, honey," I said. "It sounds like the people who were freed from prison put them up there to thank God for answering their prayers."

They were hung as ex votos, just like the silver heart, the body parts, and animals at the flea market and the boats Jessie saw in Marseille.

"I don't know," Sarah said, "Hanging chains on a church? Something's wrong about that."

"What if you thought about it in a different way?" I asked, stretching my old Sunday School muscles. "When God frees us from the bad things we've done, it's sort of like taking off a ball and chain."

As our eyes adjusted to the dim light inside the chapel, Todd whispered, "What's that face for?"

"What face?"

"You look like you're holding your breath, like you're about to go under water."

Habit, I guess. And yet as we walked around the basilica, the dread and restlessness were gone. I felt strangely light and free.

It was dark and dank, but behind the altar, mounted high on a stone pillar, was a statue of Mary in gold and silver. She sat on a chair with a miniature adult Jesus sitting on her lap, her large hands held out on each side, as if ready to catch him in case he fell. A photo in the guidebook showed the statue dressed with a crown and cape, carried high above the crowd during a pilgrimage march. "It says they still make the pilgrimage procession through the town every Ascension Sunday to the top of a nearby hill. That'd be something to see."

"Mama, Daddy," Ben cried. "Come look!" He disappeared around the corner of the transept. We followed, and there in a side chapel at one end was a roped-off aisle lined with multicolored Christmas lights.

"You won't believe what's behind that curtain!" Ben said.

"You went behind the curtain?" I asked.

"Is it Père Nöel?" Sarah asked.

"The lady said I could," Ben said. "She said it's for everyone. Here, this is where you go," he said, leading us down the aisle. He pulled aside the curtain, and we looked and gasped.

It was the most magnificent nativity scene I'd ever seen in my life, an entire mountain scene, not just a stable. It resembled the very hill and valley of Orcival.

"They're in there," Ben said, pointing to a small white house halfway up the mountain. It was lit from inside, where Mary, Joseph, and baby Jesus were; and the entire town was making its way to see the baby, each bearing a gift along the windy mountain road.

There were a few of the usual visitors: the typical shepherd and sheep, the three kings with their camels. But there were also figures I'd never seen before: men and women and children wearing work clothes or festive dresses, spilling out of other houses along the way. The blacksmith had his ironwork; the wine maker, a basket of grapes strapped to his back. A baker, a woman carrying a black hen, and a potter joined the group. Even the village idiot was there, waving his hands in the air.

"Moe, moe," Sam demanded, twisting his body down from the baby backpack toward the scene.

"See, they're all bringing gifts for Baby Jesus," said Ben.

"I know these," Sarah said. "They have a crèche like this at school. They're called santons—they make them down south in Provence. Santons—you know, like saints—but they're not saints like Joan of Arc and all those other famous ones. They're just the people in the town, and they're all bringing presents for Baby Jesus. The road has a whole town on it. Madame Bioche said that we could even be there. Daddy, you could bring a tire," she said. "Mommy, what would you bring?"

"She'd bring all her church stuff," Ben said, "and her cooler for Meals on Wheels."

"Mommy doesn't do that anymore. Right, Mommy? What would you bring?"

The question pierced me. "Well . . ."

Todd interrupted my stuttering. "She'd bring you guys. Your mommy holds us all together. Now let's go downstairs and see the crypt before Sam pulls this curtain down."

As I leaned into the rail and walked the narrow stairs, the question haunted me: What would I bring? What was I without my volunteer work? Ever since I left teaching, it was my life, trying to please God, trying to be good, while everyone else was going to work, doing what they loved—or at least searching for the job of their dreams. I'm ashamed to say that I'd thought I had the truer calling, the higher calling even. But it was just another calling. Or was it even my calling at all? Did I do it only to earn God's love?

Part of the reason I loved my service work was because I'd found that what Jesus said was true: "Whatever you do to the least of these, you do unto me." I really had found Jesus in the disadvantaged kids I tutored, in my Meals on Wheels clients, in the kids and the teachers at school. I loved those people, even if part of my motivation was to earn God's approval.

The blacksmith, the baker, the crazy man in the crèche—they were out in the world, being the people God had made them to be. They weren't chaining themselves to the church.

Chaining themselves to the church . . . ? A stone dropped in the pit of my stomach—the shackles with the balls and chains. When I saw them my first thought was bondage: that's one way to keep people in church. God hadn't put those chains on me; I'd done it myself. I came to France set free, but I kept running back to the church where it was safe, trying to re-chain myself.

Now that there were no church programs to chain myself to, I had found God in places I'd never noticed before, as close as a shadow. And I'd found him in everyone, in Cindy and Jessie and Barbara and the strangers at the flea market. I'm sure he was in the other women at school too, if I made an effort to get to know them. Had the chains kept me from making that effort? Was I using church to hide from the rest of the world?

As they tiptoed around the crypt, I prayed a silent prayer: Take those chains off me, please God. I don't want them.

You put them on. Take them off yourself.

Was that God or my own conscience talking? What if I walked away from church for a while, to find out what God had for me in other places? Cindy left church, but she had a Bible study to fall back on. I didn't have that. Church had always been the center of my world. Even if it had grown empty to me, I wasn't sure I could leave it. What if I found out that I liked playing hooky? What if I didn't go back?

I would add the ancient chains and shackles of Orcival to my collection of wonders and saints deserving a holy card of their own.

I'd draw them as they were, bolted on the side of their Romanesque basilica, above the great wooden doors. I'd draw the doors open, with snow blowing in. You could walk in, but you could also leave.

The tagline would be easy:

For freedom, Christ has set us free.

As I stepped out those doors into the cold, pausing under the shackles and chains as if they were mistletoe inviting me to kiss any hint of imprisonment goodbye, I prayed the prayer I'd write on the back:

God, who sets the prisoners free, keep us from chaining ourselves to anything but you. As we make our way on our own broken roads to your side, remind us that the gift you really want is ourselves, our own hearts, which you make sacred with your love. Strengthen our trust to walk in freedom, hands free, knowing you are as close to us as a shadow.

Ben jumped down the steps and held his face up to the falling snow, licking it with his tongue. "Look," Sarah shouted, spinning with her arms outstretched, "we're in a snow globe!" We were. God had turned over his crystal cup of sky, catching us in it, tiny figures beside the dark Notre Dame d'Orcival, with another man too, a stranger, the collar of his coat turned up against the weather, walking briskly from the boulangerie across the street, the windows golden with light.

"Anybody want a pain au chocolat?" Todd asked, and the kids cheered. Even in my unease I had to notice how eerily beautiful it all was—the stranger, the snow, and the messy tracks we made across its pure whiteness. As the man lifted his eyes to ours and nodded, I imagined God's fingers reaching down to pinch the nape of his collar, lifting him out of the snow globe, and into the crèche, onto the santon road with the rest of his village, making his way toward Christ.

God, could I come too?

But there was only the laughter of my children as they shuffled their way across the street and the soft tapping of snow white manna falling at my feet.

Chapter 18
I Sing Because I'm Happy

If I really was supposed to step into freedom away from the church, at least for a little while, surely God didn't mean for me to skip the Christmas Eve pageant; to miss seeing the performances of my angel, shepherd, and little wandering lamb. Besides, it seemed the perfect service to push the pause button on my time at Christ Church.

As my children welcomed Baby Jesus into the world, I could say goodbye to the Boy Jesus in the stained glass. *Au revoir, Jésus*, at least for a few weeks. Hopefully I'd be back.

The pageant's first and only rehearsal started a half hour before the service was to begin, and as we walked into the chapel I almost laughed at the sight. Mary was chewing bubble gum and bobby-pinning a dishcloth to her head, the three kings were playing Monkey in the Middle with the frankincense, and two angels were arguing over a set of wings.

I handed Sarah the halo from my purse, tightened Ben's bathrobe sash, and they hurried to join the group. As Todd followed Sam around the chapel, I looked up at Boy Jesus in the window. The winter sun was setting; he was fading fast.

When I'd told Todd about my intended break from church a few days ago, he put down his book and promised to do a better job taking charge of Sam.

"No, that's not it. It's not just about Sam," I said, admitting it out loud for the first time.

"What is it then?" he said. "I thought you were happy."

"You know I'm happy here. I love our life. That's the problem. I'm happy everywhere but . . ." I bit my lip. Could I say it? "I'm happy everywhere but church. But it's not Christ Church's fault."

It was church, period. I'd always thought I'd gone to worship God, but now I had to face facts. I went for me too, as a refuge from the rest of the world, a culture with rules that made sense to me, where I could lead and earn my place with God—when the truth was that I didn't need to earn anything at all.

"It's church then? OK, I get it. It's nothing like First Baptist, I know . . ."

"No, the service is fine."

"Well, what is it?"

I folded my arms in front of me. "I'm not sure."

"OK," he said, trying to read my eyes. "If you need a break for a while, I can take the big kids on my own. I do wish you'd talk to me about it, though."

I'd always shared everything, but this I held close. He didn't push me to explain. Maybe he could see that something big was brewing in my head, something that I needed space to work out myself. He kept a close eye on Sammy, which wasn't easy.

Not two minutes after the rehearsal began, Sam barged into the scene, heading straight for the manger. Moms and dads laughed as he snatched up Baby Jesus by a foot and turned quick to see if anyone would stop him. Todd picked Sam up, being careful not to trip over the donkey, and tried to wrestle Baby Jesus out of his grip. I laughed along with everyone else. I loved my husband so.

Finally the children filed out, everyone sat down, and the pageant began. I was shocked to find that I had no need to fidget, no urge to get up and run out the door. Maybe I was getting better and didn't need to step away.

"Fear not," the angel said, breaking into my thoughts. Madame Pink Suit had said the same thing in my dream as she offered me the bread, holy nourishment for my soul. Could my sabbatical from church feed my spirit as well?

As Shepherd Ben neared our pew, sniffling his way down the aisle toward the holy family, I sneaked him a tissue for the pocket of his robe. If only I could pass him my shackles too, and he could lay them on the altar as my gift to God. I'm giving them up, Lord, I prayed. I promise I won't hide here anymore, or make this place my ladder for success. I want to be free to find you everywhere.

As the shepherds gathered around the baby, my mind wandered back to Orcival again, back to the santons' path. The shepherds were the first ones journeying to Christ—like the blacksmith on the mountain road, the grape picker, and the potter—not the priest or the church Volunteer of the Year. Could I be a shepherd too?

Christmas vacation was deliciously peaceful. We stayed in our pajamas until after lunch every day, the kids played with their new toys, and Todd and I sat and drank coffee and talked. We chatted on the phone with our family and grazed on more cheese and bread and saucisson than we needed. Finally it came time for the only event on our calendar: La Nuit du Gospel.

It would just be the five of us, unfortunately. Amelie called and said that Christophe and Marthe had come down with a virus, so we'd have to go alone. I was disappointed. My French was finally improving, and I'd looked forward to getting to know her better.

"Are you sure this is the right place?" I asked as we walked out of the parking garage.

Todd nodded. How could I have never noticed the *Église St. Pierre Les Minimes*, right on Clermont's most traveled square? I couldn't help feeling sorry for it, with its flat, unornamented, stone face. Of all the neighborhood churches, *Notre Dame de l'Assomption*, Clermont's gothic cathedral, and *Notre Dame du Port*, the eleventh-century Romanesque basilica and UNESCO World Heritage Site, it was the ugly stepsister.

As the former monastery for the *Pères Minimes,* the Lesser Fathers, the austerity made sense. Maybe this was the perfect place. Gospel music didn't fill the fanciest churches or opera houses. It played more humble places and tapped into a spirit much wilder than the refined could handle.

The mob grew. Who knew that the French would be so curious about gospel music? Maybe they felt the same thirst I felt, mired in their reserved, measured behavior. A single church door opened, and the crowd pushed forward. I struggled to keep hold of Ben as my stomach filled with butterflies. Did the singers know what they were getting into? Would the French respond to the music?

At least one French person would. Matilde, a redhead who worked with my hairdresser, had made a point to tell me about the concert and to say that she would be there. "I've bought my ticket," she'd said at my last haircut. She'd grown up listening to Mahalia Jackson, and even though she couldn't understand all the words, the music was pure joy to her. "Do you realize that it came from roots of slavery?" she asked.

I nodded.

"They found their freedom in God. I ask you, who can resist such contagious joy?"

With everyone in the salon staring at me, all I could manage was "Yes, I agree."

As we entered the sanctuary and found our seats, I scanned the pews for her. Everyone was dressed in the Clermont black, filling the pews, but careful not to sit too close to one another.

The lights finally dimmed—twenty-two minutes after the concert's supposed start time. My heart skipped a beat as five men and women walked onto the stage in the darkness. I worried for them. Had they ever performed in France? Would they be disappointed?

I looked at the man next to me, at the line of his mouth turning down in a frown. It wasn't his fault—he might be a perfectly cheerful man as French men go, but he was trained to hold back enthusiasm.

I watched the silhouettes getting in place and wished them well. The crowd hushed to a silence. The singers stepped up to their microphones, and I caught one of them glancing at another. Were they waiting on an introduction?

The lights went out and then flashed back on in red and blue, revealing three women and two men in choir robes, their heads bowed. Suddenly chords bubbled out of the organ, drums joined in, the singers stepped up to their microphones, and "Down by the Riverside" rolled out of their bodies like a storm, with thunder and lightning. The choir rocked in waves, back and forth, shaking their tambourines, singing their hearts out, and stirring up a gospel tornado spinning to the rooftop of the seventeenth-century church.

I could feel the power and emotion of their voices reverberating in my own bones. Is that what drew the French, too?

Todd and I looked at each other and laughed out loud in amazement, not that anyone could hear us. The French looked stunned, frozen in their pews as if the rush of sound had turned them into stone.

Finally, at the second verse, one lady in the third pew from the front stood up and started swaying awkwardly to the music, like Pinocchio come to life.

I got goose bumps when they sang "Motherless Child" and nearly wept at "His Eye Is on the Sparrow."

"Why should I feel discouraged, why should the shadows come? . . . His eye is on the sparrow, and I know He watches me."

They started the chorus: "I sing because I'm happy, I sing because I'm free" . . . and it came to me.

Freedom! That's what this was. I'd taken off the shackles of church, of all my rules about whom I could learn from (everyone) and whom God loved best (no one.) It was time to celebrate it, live it! I had my own choir backing me up—Clotilde and Madame Pink Suit, even the singer in Ambert, joining in like a human bell.

The choir started in on "O When the Saints," and I had to wipe a few more tears away, picturing them all in a conga line of nobodies—holy nobodies—dancing up the hill of Orcival with the flea market crowd, hoisting Mary and Jesus high above their heads.

An old woman at the front stood up, slipped off her coat, and joined in the dancing. Two more joined her, opening themselves to the spirit, to words they might not even understand.

Why couldn't I respond to God like that . . . to my life like that? Why did everything I do have to be so planned and perfect? Why did I wrap myself up with chains when God held out his hands to help me?

I started clapping, not caring if I was the only one on our pew doing so. The kids laughed at first, but soon the whole family was clapping along—even Sam, who'd stopped playing with the small toys we'd brought, entranced by the show on the stage.

By the time they got to the last verse, a few more people were joining in, clapping deliberately, holding their arms at an erect angle, as if their hands were cymbals. Many couldn't help smiling, their eyes jumping at every trill of the voice and shake of the tambourine. Matilde was right. The freedom was contagious.

A young woman in sequins sang "Amazing Grace," and tears came again. I blinked them back, shocked at the truth of the song I'd sung so many times. I'd felt like such a wretch, spending my life trying to be good, trying to earn God's approval. I'd even tricked my mind into thinking that's how it was supposed to be. But France was bathing me in beauty and leisure and gave me time to think about the feelings I'd always pushed aside.

I didn't have to earn anything here. I couldn't earn anything! It was all free. Wasn't that what grace was about, being doused in God's love without earning it? It was for everyone, for the people dancing, not even understanding the words, even if they'd just come for the music.

I watched them sway to the music, feeling myself move along. Could I serve God like that, just feeling my way for a while away from church? Trusting that grace would lead me home?

The singers finished the hymn and stepped back into the darkness, but the organ continued with another verse, playing it in the background as a man in a rhinestone suit stepped forward and started to preach. Didn't he know that these people didn't speak English?

The audience started to murmur as he began his message, saying that God had given us Creation, by creating us; Exodus, by freeing us; and Resurrection, in the eternal life of the risen Lord. Todd and I looked at each other. The audience was getting restless. Sweat began beading on the preacher's forehead. But still he preached, ignoring the chatter.

"*Chant!*" (Sing!) shouted a man in the back of the church.

Sarah whipped her head around, looking to see who spoke. "That's so rude," she whispered.

"But they're frustrated. They can't understand him," I said.

Finally the music changed, his backup singers stepped into the light, and he began the first verse of "Go Tell It on the Mountain." Instantly the crowd was back on his side. He'd tried to lead them with his words when all they understood was the power of his song.

He took the microphone from its stand and stepped off the stage into the aisle nearest us, and people began straining in their pews to see where he was walking, reaching out to shake his hand. That's it, I wanted to say to him; that's what they want: for you to be with them, not above them. We're all holy nobodies.

Maybe the lesson was for me too: to be with the people around me; to acknowledge my own failings and disappointments along with the goodness of God. Maybe Madame Pink Suit and the conga line of wayward saints was God's way of shouting "Chant!" to me. Sing, Becky! We're all in this together. Sing!

By the time the last group took to the microphones, the crowd had loosened up so much that a total of eight people (eight!) were now standing and dancing. A couple dozen were clapping along, and a few heads even bobbed to the music.

A man in a white robe took the microphone off the stand and walked down the center aisle. "We come from Martinique," he said in French, "to share God's love with you." The audience clapped, thrilled to understand him. "Love gives us freedom," he said in French. "Can I get an 'Amen'?"

There was a pause, and then there was a lone "Amen" from the back of the room.

Everyone laughed and turned around to look.

"That's right," the man said, putting a hand to his forehead. "I'd forgotten. We're in France. You don't do that: my apologies."

He returned to the stage. "You know, in the Bible it says 'It is for freedom that Christ has set us free. Stand firm, then, and do not let yourselves be burdened again by a yoke of slavery.' Well, Mesdames and Messieurs, I want you to set yourself free and I'm going to help you do it."

He smiled, as if he had a joke to tell. "We're all on the road together, and we need each other. So I want you to do something for me. I want you to reach out your arms like this and hold the hands of your neighbors."

Everyone laughed, their hands in their laps, waiting for the punch line.

"Go ahead," the man laughed. "You can do it."

I looked to the man down the pew from me, and he gave me a sheepish smile.

"My people, I know this is not natural for you," he said, at which the crowd laughed again, "but God can help you. Go ahead now. Go on!"

The man on my pew and I looked nervously at each other again and laughed. I reached out my hand. He took it, in a soft, weak grasp.

"See, that wasn't too hard, was it?" the singer said.

My new neighbor dropped my hand.

"I didn't say we were finished. Hold the person's hand and look into their eyes and say 'I love you, my brother. I love you, my sister.'"

There was silence, then laughter. We grasped hands again, and this time the man held firm, his hand warm and strong.

"God, help them in their weakness," the man in the robe prayed, smiling.

My neighbor looked at me and laughed nervously. "I love you, my sister."

I smiled. "Merci, monsieur. And I love you too."

He smiled back, his eyes sparkling. He nodded at the boys, asleep on the pew between me and Todd. "How do they sleep during this?" he asked.

"I don't know," I smiled, shrugging my shoulders.

"Children are like angels," he said.

I started to say "yes, when they're sleeping," but stopped myself. It was too holy a moment to be the least bit cynical. Besides, it was true. There in my pew I felt surrounded by angels, a heavenly host of strangers, men and women and children too.

I'd capture these saints, these strangers, these brothers and sisters in Christ or at least in song, on my newest holy card, each wearing angel wings, to mark them as God's. It didn't matter if they'd earned it or not. We couldn't really earn anything anyway. God loved them no matter what, as they sat there or swayed or clapped their hands like cymbals.

I'd add the tagline:

"Chant!"

And the prayer?

Giver of amazing grace, you created us to need each other, God,. help us in our weaknesses to reach across the aisle and hold hands. Help us sing and dance with you, Lord, celebrating the freedom only you can give.

As we walked into the night sky, I watched the angels disperse across the courtyard, into city streets and down into the underground parking lot, back to their cars and motorbikes, heading home all across the city and into the villages. The stars twinkled on the streets before them, the moonlight shone down on their shoulders, and God breathed his spirit over their heads and hearts as they made their way home— their souls still swaying to the love songs of the evening.

Chapter 19
Treasure Hunt

The first time I sent my family to church without me, I felt alarmingly happy. As Todd shepherded the kids into the car, I tried my best to look grim.

"I still don't think it's fair," Ben said. "You and Sam get to stay home from church, and you aren't even sick."

He's right, my conscience whispered. "Honey, I'm not going to explain this again. Sam and I are going to have church here."

Ben wasn't the only one who'd ask questions. The expat ladies would want to know who was sick. "Just tell them it's because of Sam, that it's just too hard to keep him quiet right now," I'd told Todd.

Todd had said he would. We both knew Sam wasn't the only reason I was skipping out, but maybe it'd buy me some privacy for a while. He kissed me through the open window and whispered in my ear, "Weird New Year's resolution if you ask me—to play more hooky from church."

"Very funny," I said, and kissed the kids goodbye.

"Listen to Daddy," I said. "If you're good, he'll stop on the way home from church and pick up pizza, and we'll have another king's cake for dessert."

Ben folded his arms and grunted.

"Unless you don't like king's cake anymore," I said.

"That'd be fine I guess," he answered.

As I closed the door behind me with Sam on my hip, I felt a surge of bliss. What a glorious Sabbath I'd had already, and now there'd be no chasing after Sam, no trying to keep him quiet with toys or crackers. He was completely free to be himself—to run and yell to his heart's content, and I was free as well.

I could have my own worship service inside my head and do it however I liked: sing the hymns of my own choosing, read scripture, or just pray—whatever came to me. I wanted the Sabbath that the rhinestone man had preached about: worship as the living symbol of the Christian story, Genesis, Exodus, and Resurrection, all rolled up into one. I'd already enjoyed the Genesis part, spending my morning in re-creation.

I had gone to the flea market all by myself, strode the aisles in the cold rain, sloshing through puddles in my boots, talking to the vendors, taking in the treasures and the everyday things as well, which had begun to feel holy to me. Everyone seemed to have a basket of *fèves* on their tables, the little porcelain figures baked into king's cakes. Of course they did. It was Epiphany Sunday. We were right in the heart of king's cake season.

I remembered the first time I saw a fève at the flea market, back in the days before I'd ever imagined leaving church. I thought it was the French version of a Polly Pocket, the plastic doll slightly taller than a fingernail that, thanks to Sarah, our vacuum cleaner sucked up on a regular basis. No, on closer inspection it was a tiny porcelain angel with blond flowing hair, a painted blue gown, and had the words L'Ange Gabriel printed at its feet.

"It's the Angel Gabriel," I said.

"Wait," said Cindy. "Wasn't Gabriel a man angel? That one's got boobs and red lipstick!"

The vendor behind the table saw us, pointed at Cindy with her cigarette, and murmured something I couldn't understand.

"*Répétéz, s'il vous plaît?*" Cindy asked.

"Oh you're foreigners," the vendor said, slowing her French. She handed Cindy the basketful of tiny china figures. "Are you looking for one in particular?"

"No, I'm just looking."

"Ah, well, allow me to explain. These are fèves, the little china figures used in the *galette des Rois* (king's cake) for Epiphany. The baker puts one or two in every cake, and whoever gets the fève in their portion gets to be the king or queen and wear the crown. They used to be religious—you know, Jesus, Mary, Joseph. But now that France has gone to hell, they're most anything."

She took the basket back from Cindy's hands. "What do we have here?" she inquired, picking through them. "Let's see . . . Jesus, Jesus, Jesus . . . Ah! Look, an éclair. See?"

She picked it up, and I examined it. The holy éclair!

"Oh, you like that one, do you? Here's the wolf from 'Little Red Riding Hood' . . . hmm."

The lady picked out a round one and frowned at the yellow smiley face printed on it. "I don't know what this is . . . maybe an idiot? Oh here's a British man—you might like that one. They do series, you know, of different countries or professions. Here's Tarzan. Last year I started getting all these Disney characters—ugh. The Americans are getting into everything—entirely too many of those."

Now that Epiphany had come and gone, we'd amassed quite a collection of fèves ourselves. In addition to the baby Jesus I'd bought from the cigarette lady, we'd eaten enough galettes to supply two more baby Jesuses, a horseshoe, a Mary, a baker, an éclair, the Leaning Tower of Pisa, Balthazar, a shepherd, a wolf, a trout, and an idiot (smiley face) to the collection.

They were so much more interesting than the plastic baby Jesus hidden inside the New Orleans style king's cake we'd had at children's church back in South Carolina. Next to the tiny French Jésus, the American Jesus was Incredible Hulk Baby. "That was probably to make sure so no one would choke on it," Sarah added, shaking her head in disgust. "You know how Americans like to sue."

Luckily no one had choked so far, and they'd had plenty of chances. The day after the gospel concert my new friend Colette invited us over and served us our first taste of the galette des Rois, and Todd and I looked at each other in awe. How could we have lived our whole lives without *frangipane*, the buttery almond filling that made me nearly cry with joy? The kids thought it was delicious, but they were more excited about the ritual that went with the cake.

Ben and Sarah became the Galette Police, insisting we follow each step of the custom the exact French way. I'd warm the cake in the oven, and as I carried it into the dining room, Ben would scoot underneath the table, yanking Sam under with him. As I cut each piece, the youngest child was supposed to choose which person to give it to, just to keep things fair in case the fève was sticking out in plain sight.

Sam had no idea what to do, but he was happy to be the star of the show, echoing Ben's words in a happy shout. Once everyone was served, the boys would pop back up, we'd stick Sam back in his high chair, and Ben would take a seat. They'd wait for my signal and then dig in, searching for the fève as Todd and I took our time, savoring each morsel.

I'd bought another cake for dessert tonight. The frangipane and puff pastry might thrill my taste buds, but its symbolism excited the believer in me. I especially loved that it put a child in charge, as God so often seems wont to do, and that we were led in a physical search for the Babe, just as the Magi had done.

Now as I sang another hymn and arranged our collection of fèves, it occurred to me what a bittersweet symbol they made of my religious journey in France, my search for Jesus hidden within this delicious French life. He was always showing up in unexpected places:

. . . in my friends who skipped out on church

. . . in the linen lady at the market

. . . in the crying man in Ambert

. . . in the last geranium petals falling down from window boxes and in the cold rain that washed them down the street

. . . in the rituals that made my Baptist self uncomfortable

. . . in the recited creed and prayers

. . . in the bread and the chalice, even when Sam or my inner voice seemed bent on disrupting the worship of Christ Church.

Christ Church . . . Worship was more than halfway over by now. I haven't even read any scripture.

So if I'd already experienced recreation, feeling renewed and in love with God in the quietness of my Sunday, what about Exodus?

Honey, you're living it.

Was it blasphemous to compare playing hooky from church to freedom from slavery? But after so many years of being blindly obedient to my church calendar, maybe I needed an exodus of my own, to see what was lurking for me in the wilderness. My self-imposed shackles had made me sore.

And Resurrection . . . ? Where was the risen Savior in all of this?

I sat on the floor, rolling the ball back and forth with Sammy, and prayed a silent prayer, relieved almost to tears to find that my words didn't bounce off the walls but were somehow received, settled, caught. I looked at the shutters bolted shut. Maybe I should try reading the Bible again. There'd be no breeze tickling the back of my neck, no neighbors' conversations to translate, no rain knocking at the glass, calling me away from the page.

I took my Bible off the shelf. Was I on the right track, or was skipping church just giving in to my own laziness, a lack of spiritual discipline?

I'd start with something easy, something I knew by heart. I turned the pages to Psalm 139.

"Lord, you have examined me and you know me. You know everything I do."

My eyes jumped all over the page as I read the words from memory. It's OK. This is new again. It might take a while to concentrate.

"From far away you understand all my thoughts."

Wasn't this font different from the font in my New Revised Standard? God, help me concentrate.

"You see me, whether I am working or resting;"

There's Katie. Did I scoop her litter box already? Stop it!

"You know all my actions."

Blah, blah, blah . . . let's skip to the good part.

"Where could I go to escape from you?"

I'm thirsty. Sit back down. You're not trying very hard.

"Where could I get away from your presence?"

My own living room . . . Why was this so hard?

"If I went up to heaven, you would be there. If I lay down in the world of the dead, you would be there."

Am I lazy? Out of the habit?

"If I flew away beyond the east"

My legs are hurting. Maybe if I don't sit on them . . .

"or lived in the farthest place in the west, You would be there to lead me, you would be there to—"

Enough of this . . . I put my Bible back on the shelf. It wasn't working. I was praying again. Why couldn't I read? The Bible had always been my rock. I'd read it nearly daily my entire adult life. But maybe I was pushing too much. I had connected to God through my prayers. That was a start. It doesn't have to be perfect, I reminded myself.

A few minutes later Todd's keys jingled in the door. Resurrection would have to wait.

"So how was the sermon?" I asked, following him into the kitchen with the pizzas.

"It was really good. Father Joe talked about new beginnings—"

"Who was there?"

"The normal crowd."

"Did anyone ask where I was?" I asked, slicing the pizzas.

"Frances asked if Sam was sick, and I told them he wasn't. I said that you were going to keep him home for a while."

"What'd she say?"

"Nothing," Todd shrugged his shoulders. "Nobody said anything."

"Nobody?"

"Well . . . maybe Stephanie said something. I can't really remember."

I knew it. I was sure Stephanie would have something to say. It wasn't that she was judgmental. Stephanie really wasn't that way—at least she didn't mean to be. Her family had moved to Clermont in November and, by the sound of it, I was pretty sure she had been as involved in church as I was—or used to be. So far they'd never missed a Sunday.

"Are you sure you can't remember what she said?"

"She was nice about it, Beck. She just said something like you should get real; that all kids make noise and nobody cares."

"She said I should get real?"

"No, I said it wrong. Her point was that you shouldn't worry about Sam's noise."

"That's easy for her to say. Her kids sit there like zombies. I've never heard that baby make a single noise. He just sits there sucking on his pacifier."

Todd nodded.

"You know I can't concentrate in there with Sam running around.

And right now is just not a good time—"

"I get it, Beck. You don't have to convince me. Nobody thinks badly of you, if that's what you're afraid of."

"I'm not afraid of anything."

As I sliced the pizza and Todd poured drinks, I tried to put Stephanie's comment in perspective. I might have said the same thing. But I knew staying home was right for me at this time. Hadn't I decided to try new things, to put on the pink suit for a while, hop on the moped and see what works for me? It was my journey, no matter what anyone thought. I couldn't put on the chains again. It felt too good to be free. If and when I returned to church with the same fervor, it would be with no shoulds, no ought-to's, and not before I was ready.

A few minutes later, as I brought the galette to the table, Ben scooted underneath and Sam followed after him, giggling. I cut through the layers of puff pastry scored in diamonds, as the sweet scent of butter and almonds filled the room.

"Here," Todd said, "let me help you with that."

I distracted Sarah as he peeked under the pastry top for each slice, as we always did, to make sure that one of the kids received the fève.

Ben called out the names, and I passed the plates.

One by one they all searched their slices, eyeing the sides and lifting the top crust. Where was the fève? Had the chef forgotten it?

I took a bite and felt something hard chink against my tooth. I fished it out of my mouth as everyone stared. "Mommy, it's you!" Ben cheered. It was a tiny white lamb with black dots for eyes and a pink smile.

"How about that?" Todd commented, in feigned surprise.

"Yeah," Ben added, "Mommy never gets the fève!"

"Here, Mommy, sit still," said Sarah, fastening the strip of the paper garland into a crown. "You know we have to go through the whole ritual. We have to get it right."

As she crowned me queen, everyone clapped and laughed.

Sarah's word "ritual" echoed in my ear, letting loose a stream of images: the Eucharist at church, my end table set with three candles before I put them back in the kitchen, Mary Margaret crossing herself before approaching the altar table.

And now the cake, the fève, more ritual for my journey.

I stood the little lamb up at the head of my plate for everyone to see, my Lamb of God, given freely to me all day long—even if I couldn't drum up the patience to read ten verses of a psalm I'd memorized for years, even if I hadn't earned it in any way.

Sam threw his arms toward me, and I pulled him onto my lap. As Ben and Sarah talked at once, I fingered the lamb . . . the Lamb of God, who takes away the sin of the world. I'd put it on my newest holy card, along with the galette des Rois, with its golden puff pastry crust and buttery almond frangipane, and the paper crown it came with and the table set for our celebration.

I knew at once what the tagline would be:

Taste and see that the Lord is good!

And the prayer?

> Dear God, who sends a child to lead us, be with us as we search for Jesus, to make him king of our hearts. Thank you for hiding within plain sight, within wonders and saints both savory and sweet, so that we must look to find you. And when the tables turn and we hide from you, God, thank you for journeying into the wild and looking until every lost sheep is back in the fold. We wear your crown, Lord, to celebrate your risen life within us.

I might be bumbling through the wilderness, but thanks be to God, it was God's wilderness, and he would be there to lead me. I remembered that Psalm 139 said so, even if I couldn't get through the whole thing.

Chapter 20
Prayers in Paint

At 11:22 on a school night I stood in the entryway of my house, slipping on a coat over my nightgown.

"What are you doing out there?" Todd called from the bedroom. "Do you know what time it is?"

"I left something in the car," I said. "You know how she is."

Todd immediately understood. Thanks to Madame Mallet, we were on constant surveillance. If we brought home anything unusual, it was easier to sneak it in under the cover of darkness than to face her barrage of questions.

When I lugged a large canvas into our bedroom and unloaded a bagful of brushes and oil paints onto the dresser, Todd sat up in bed.

"What in the world?"

I laughed.

"But you don't even paint!"

"I know!" I said. "It's funny, isn't it?"

"Let me guess," he said. "You've been hanging out with Jessie again."

He was right. That very morning Jessie and I had ended up strolling the babies downtown to the art supply store so that she could pick up a couple of tubes of paint, and somehow I walked out with an armload of supplies of my own. "I promise you'll love it!" she'd said. "You won't believe how easy it is."

She didn't have to twist my arm. I'd always wanted to paint, and now I certainly had the time. Ever since I'd unchained myself from church, I'd traded the shackles for a "What Would Madame Pink Suit Do?" bracelet. The answer was obvious. She'd say, "Fear not and get out the brushes."

Why couldn't I try on the artist's smock for a while? I'd worn one back in my teenage years, when I filled a sketchbook with drawings of my foot and anything else that would sit still long enough to pose for me.

"You've got to try painting," Jessie had said. "You're in France, after all."

So I bought the whole set-up. What was the worst that could happen? If I flopped at being an *artiste*, at least Ben and Sarah would get new art supplies.

On the way back to our cars, Jessie invited me over. "I can help you get started. What else are you going to do . . . laundry?"

I wished I could. Stephanie had already asked me to lunch at her house, "to let the babies play"—at least that's what she'd said. I tried to be positive, but I was pretty sure I knew what she wanted. Since I stayed home from church on Sunday and no one was even sick, I must be suffering some kind of spiritual crisis. A few months ago I might have said the same thing to someone, hoping to be helpful.

I did appreciate that she cared. None of the other expats talked about faith much outside of church, and I liked the openness she had about it. She talked about her prayer life in the same way she chatted about her favorite French pastry or her son's allergy to milk.

"I'm so glad you came," she said as we fed the babies at her kitchen table.

"We missed you at church on Sunday."

"Thanks. You know I'd like to be there," I said, wishing that the words could make it true. "But with Sam as active as he is, we're just going to take a break for a while. I just do my own worship at home."

Stephanie tilted her head, considering it. "It's nice that no matter where we are, God is always available."

"It *was* really nice. I enjoyed the quiet."

"I bet." Stephanie took a sip of her water. "But you know, Becky, nobody cares if Sam makes noise. You should see Jacob in church. He's wild as can be."

I glanced at Jacob. He was sitting in his high chair perfectly still, his hands in his lap, waiting open-mouthed for the next spoonful of applesauce while Sam bounced in his clip-on seat, rubbing carrots into his eyebrows.

"I know nobody cares," I said. "It's really about me, not him."

Stephanie took a bite of her salad. Should I tell her the whole truth?

"This might sound weird," I said, "but right now I feel like God is leading me away from church."

"Leading you away from church? Why would God do that? That doesn't make sense."

"I know it sounds crazy, but I'm beginning to think it's true. When I get in line for communion or try to pray, I just can't concentrate. I'm tired of going through the motions. At least if I stay home with Sam, Todd and the kids can worship in peace."

"But don't you think it's worth it just to go through the motions? You know God can make something valuable out of your attempts at worship, even when all you can do is show up."

I took a bite of bread. She wanted me to pretend to worship when my mind was somewhere else? An alarm went off in my brain. Going through the motions, following ritual just for ritual's sake . . . Was that a good thing?

My brain turned on its slide show again: the candles, Mary Margaret crossing herself. OK, maybe there was worth in going through the motions, up to a point. But why couldn't God lead me away from church? Why wouldn't that be possible?

"God values our discipline," Stephanie said, "and our obedience."

So I was being disobedient? This conversation was over. I should have gone home with Jessie.

"Besides," she went on, "I think consistent attendance at church is a good witness for our children and for other people. My kids embarrass me too sometimes, but I've come to realize—it's taken me a long time—that sometimes I have to put God ahead of my kids. You know what I mean?"

I tried not to physically bristle. Hadn't I spent enough of my life trying to be a good example, worrying about my witness and what other people thought? Wasn't it time they decided things for themselves and left me out of it?

"Becky, I've found that when I put God first, things always seem to fall into place."

Easy, now. I took another bite. You owe her no explanation. I took a sip of water. I should be at Jessie's.

"But of course it's your decision."

I nodded and paused to find the right words. "I think that for me, Stephanie, keeping Sam home is the right thing to do at this time. But I appreciate your concern."

After we cleaned everything up from lunch I looked at my watch. "I'm sorry, but I've got to run."

"What? Did you forget something?" she laughed. "You've been hanging around Jessie too much."

I scooped Sam onto my hip. I had heard Stephanie laugh about Jessie's absentmindedness before and thought it was a bit mean-spirited. "I've got an appointment I need to get to."

"An appointment . . . Are you OK?"

"It's not for the doctor," I said. "I'm taking art lessons. Jessie said she'd teach me."

"Really? That's great," Stephanie said, a little too eagerly, and walked me to the door. "Um, I hope you don't get the wrong idea—I didn't mean to say anything bad about Jessie. I love her—she's just . . . you know how creative people are."

I nodded. Jessie was a creative soul. She might not know it yet, but she was my new *professeur d'arte*. It was time for Lesson Number One.

Jessie opened the door with her sweater on inside out and paint all over her fingers.

"You came to paint! I knew you wanted to do it!"

"If it's OK with you—if you're not too busy."

"Busy? Are you kidding? This is great. Abby was getting bored while I was working. Now she and Sam can play."

Joan of Arc was on the credenza, staring into the dining room. Today Joan seemed noble—the intensity of her eyes, her pretty armored feet, the way she clung to her shield—not hiding behind it, but thrusting it forward as a weapon.

"Joan looks great there."

"Doesn't she? I just love her. Sometimes I'll look over at her while I'm working and I just have to stop and admire her. Honestly, she's the best thing I've got."

"Jessie, there's . . . um . . . you've got something on your sweater," I reached up and pulled on it. "Oh, it's the tag."

"What?" she said, reaching around to feel it.

"I think you've got it on inside out."

She laughed. "I guess I got caught up in my work. You'll see. That happens sometimes. You can get really lost in it, because you're working so hard to see what you're painting, trying to really look into it."

What in the world was she talking about?

"But first," Jessie said, "coffee."

As Jessie made the espressos, she nodded at the book of van Gogh paintings on her kitchen table.

"Take a look at that. One of those might be perfect to get you started. They're really easy to copy."

"There are so many," I said, flipping through the pages. "It's kind of overwhelming."

"Why don't you look around at the ones I've done? Maybe one of them will speak to you."

Jessie's walls were covered with paintings—maybe a dozen of them, mostly van Goghs. There was the one of his bedroom, child-like in simplicity with playful colors, the haystack one with the couple napping, the village scene with a curvy road and crooked houses, and a painting I'd never seen before: a somber, hulking church, sitting on a village hill under a foreboding sky. A road approached and forked around it, as if trying to avoid it.

Jessie brought me my coffee as I stared at it. "You like that one?"

I nodded. "It's beautiful. But the church looks sort of . . . scary . . . abandoned."

"Yeah," Jessie nodded. "It's funny: van Gogh started out as an evangelist, a preacher like his dad and his uncles, but he clearly had conflicting feelings about the church. What about this one?" she asked, walking over to the large painting behind the couch. "I think it's my favorite."

I recognized the painting. It was *The Starry Night*, except it was different.

"Is that the church downtown?"

"Uh huh," Jessie responded. "I like to personalize the paintings, put my own signature on them if I can."

She had replaced van Gogh's silhouetted church with the

cathedral of Clermont, the moonlight bouncing off its twin spires. It was stunning—the sky rolling over the dark, sloping mountains, the glowing moon practically vibrating off the canvas, the cedar in the foreground, spiking into the sky in black flames.

"It's incredible."

"Paint it!"

I laughed. "Jessie, that's way too complicated for me. I've got to start with something simpler."

"Why? You're thinking it's harder than it is. It's just copying."

We watched the babies and talked for nearly two and a half hours. Jessie taught me about gridding off a canvas and sketching it out, square by square. She showed me how she'd gridded her current work, *The Café Terrace at Night*, first on her copy of the painting and then on her canvas, and then began copying each square, sketching it in with a charcoal pencil.

We opened up my box of paints, and she explained about paint thinner and the technique of going thick over thin. First I would start with diluted paint, just to cover the canvas and give the thicker paint something to hold to, and I'd add layer upon layer, using less paint thinner as I went. It sounded like something I could actually do, at least in theory.

When it was time to pick up the kids from school, Jessie handed me her book on the way out. "Take it home and pick one out to copy. I won't need it for a long while—I've got two other paintings in line. Once you pick out what you want to do, go ahead and grid out the painting—do it right in the book. I don't care. Then start copying. Don't be afraid to just jump right in."

As I opened the trunk for Ben and Sarah's book bags at school, Sarah saw the canvas and peeked in my shopping bag.

"What's all this for?"

"I'm going to try to make a painting for us. Ellie and Abby's mommy is helping me."

"Cool," Sarah said. "When did you become a painter?"

"Oh, I'm not really a painter," I said, suddenly self-conscious.

"If you paint, Mama," Ben said, tossing his book bag into the trunk, "then you're a painter."

Two days later I was beginning to feel like one, at least a wannabe painter, leaning over the canvas propped on our dining room table, finishing my sketch as my clock stood behind me, ticking the minutes away. Luckily Sam had been content to babysit himself, babbling from amidst a pile of stuffed animals, tossing them all over our living room floor.

I'd picked Vincent's *Chair with a Pipe*, thinking it would be a fairly simple one to try. After all, there was only a chair and part of a box, with a door in the background.

"It's really fun," I'd told Jessie on the phone. It felt so satisfying, perfecting one little square at a time, erasing my mistakes and starting again. I was good at it, which made sense as I'd spent my whole life copying, following rules, mimicking whatever teachers or church folks showed me. Jessie was right: it wasn't nearly as hard as I thought it would be. The process was methodical, like math, matching the lines and angles. It was almost soothing, like a ritual.

I could hardly wait to show my finished sketch to the kids when we got home from school.

"You did that?" Ben inquired, his mouth hanging open.

Sarah elbowed him. "Don't act so surprised," she said. "Mommy is very artistic."

Unfortunately, my confidence had faded by the next day. As I put on the first layer of paint in big sections of color—the wood yellow, the floor rust, the wall green—I was shocked to watch my sketch disappear. Wouldn't the pencil at least show through the first layer of paint? How would I add any detail when all my guidelines had vanished?

"Relax," Jessie said over the phone. "You don't need those lines anymore. You just made them to divide the first layer of color. It sounds like you're thinking too much. Try to really *look* at the chair you're working toward. Stare at it long enough and you'll see the strokes van Gogh made, the individual colors. Trust your eyes."

I hung up the phone and groaned. . . . So much for playing artist. You're a copier, not a real painter. Without my cheater pencil lines, I was stuck.

I poured myself a cup of coffee, sat down at the table, and stared at the painting in the book. Maybe I could persuade Jessie to finish it for me.

I tried to focus on her directions: Try to really look at the chair you're working toward.

What'd she mean? That if I stared at it long enough, the painting muse in the sky would zap me and I'd suddenly know what to do? Couldn't I draw out a simple sketch on top of the paint?

Stare at it long enough, she had said, and you'll see van Gogh's strokes.

OK. Let's take the front leg of the chair. It's yellow—OK, more than yellow. I could see the orange and green, the brown and mustard. I drank my coffee and stared some more. There were really only a few strokes of yellow in it. I looked a little longer and the yellow strokes weren't even yellow anymore, more like green, with tiny streaks of yellow and orange running through them. I hadn't even noticed the streaking before.

I poured more coffee, and examined the colors in the original painting's tile floor. There was even purple and red in there, and the white grout wasn't white—it was green, and in the front, aqua. And electric blue outlined some of the legs and rungs like a child's marker. And the rush seat—the green and the blue and the black and orange—my eyes could feel the texture of the straw and see where it sagged in the middle. There were single black pen marks that I hadn't even noticed that separated the chair from the door and wove the straw together at the center of the seat.

As I sat at the table with Sam for lunch I flipped through more paintings, shocked to find colors I had never noticed—that the white skin of a person was actually green or yellow or red, that there were brown hollows around the eyes and green and gray within the wrinkles. As I looked, I felt my fairy godmother clock tick faster, dancing in her corner. She's found it, she's found it. Were those colors noticeable in real life as well?

My sweater wadded up at the end of the table. It was red, but I could see black and purple and gray in the folds and shadows.

When it was time to pick up the kids I couldn't help but look for the hidden colors. Stephanie came over to talk to me, but all I could concentrate on was how the right side of her face was blue-gray in the shadow of the school gate.

For a whole week I worked on my canvas, making mistakes and getting frustrated. I'd walk away, and then I'd call Jessie.

"Stop worrying about the mistakes," she'd say. "Paint right over them. I'm telling you, Becky, those mistakes will work for you. It's the layering that'll make that chair real."

She was right! As I layered the paint for the chair's seat, it came to life. The straw began to bulge on the right and sink in the center, just like it did in van Gogh's painting.

At the end of each day Todd and the children would stand around my canvas and applaud my work, excited to see the transformation. I was more thrilled than anyone, and stayed up working on it late into the night. Whenever Sam would take a nap or be willing to keep himself occupied, I'd return to the painting. I might not be able to sit still reading ten verses of a psalm, but I could concentrate on chair legs for hours!

"What are you going to paint next?" Todd asked as we got into bed.

"I don't know: probably another van Gogh."

"You know, when you started painting I was glad to see that you were doing something just for fun. But now . . . it's really coming out great!"

"Thanks," I said. "I really am loving it." I wanted to tell him that this was more than just painting to me, but I wasn't sure that even I understood what it meant. Did it even make sense that as I painted I just felt a long-lost joy? That my painting felt like a prayer issuing out of the tip of the brush, guided by my hand, powered by my heart?

It thrilled me to see that I could make mistake after mistake and still create something beautiful. It even made me feel beautiful! The brush would slip and I'd say to myself, "Aw, look what you did, sweetheart. Bless your heart, you're trying so hard." Whatever I'd messed up could be fixed, and the fixing would make the painting even better! I'd even grown to love those mistakes.

My next holy card was obvious. I'd draw the paint, my brushes, and my half-finished copy of van Gogh's chair. As crazy as it sounded I found God in that chair, in the tile floor, in the pipe. All this time I'd thought that beauty was just an extra, something God threw in for his own pleasure, but now I felt him in it! What was that about? Did the love come from the process of the looking or the painting . . . from making mistakes or forgiving them . . . from forgiving myself?

Whatever the answers, I was having my own little Sabbath in my messy dining room, right in the middle of the week. It was a happy revelation: I'd already had Creation and Exodus and now, Resurrection! I hadn't done anything for God, and still God was blessing me!

The tagline?

Still Life with Mistakes,
Thank the Lord.

And the prayer?

Dear God, creator and crafter of all, thank you for the mistakes we make and the gift of fixing them. We are so layered, Lord, thick with blunders and effort and sweat and forgiveness. Help us look hard at each other and see every color that is there. Help us see each other as you see us: as messy works of art, beautiful in their imperfections, deserving to be seen, deserving to be understood. Help us recognize you and your beauty in everything around us, in everyone around us.

I made a pact with myself: I'd quit mourning my own mistakes and see the fixing of them as a gift. God had already forgiven me, so it seemed silly and overdramatic to keep berating myself. God loved me no matter how thick my layers were.

Chapter 21

Holy Kisses

For a February Saturday, the sweater-but-no-coat weather felt almost tropical. The sun was working overtime, thawing everything out. Todd had taken the kids with him to the grocery store so that I could put the last touches on my painting, but the bright light streaming through the lace curtains on my windows made fluttery shadows on my canvas. I might have bolted the shutters closed, but after a solid week of cold gray skies, I couldn't bear to shut out the light.

I tried setting up on my kitchen counter but found more lacy shadows. No one had cleaned up from breakfast, and there wasn't a good place to put my paints. The sun looked so warm outside. If it weren't for Madame Mallet, I'd pull out a chair and work on the balcony. But she'd call me down and want to inspect my work and give me suggestions. It was too bad. It'd do my soul good to sit in the sun.

I was about to close the shutters when I saw the Mallets' car pulling out of the driveway. I'd forgotten that they were going to their niece's house for lunch. They were leaving already?

How wonderful! I dragged two chairs onto the balcony, one to act as an easel for my painting and one for me. If I worked in the sunshine, I'd stay warm enough. The light was perfect. I mixed a little yellow ochre with the brown, dabbed my fine brush, and lifted it to the canvas.

"Rébecca!" Madame Mallet called from her open bedroom window.

Startled, I dropped the brush.

"So, you're the artiste!" she exclaimed. "When I saw you bring in your canvas in the middle of the night a few weeks ago, I figured it was for one of your little marmots."

"No, it's for me," I replied, getting up from my chair. (When did that woman sleep?) "You're not visiting your niece today?"

"That's later, after Clément gets back from the store. I want to see your painting. Bring it down." She disappeared for the stairs.

We kissed each other good morning, and she yanked it out of my hands.

"Well, well! That's not bad at all!" she said, looking it over. "Rébecca, it's not bad at all! It's a van Gogh, isn't it?"

I nodded, pleased with her approval.

"Of course I don't care for van Gogh myself, but you've done a good job copying it. What will you do to make it yours?"

"Répétez?"

"I said, 'What will you do to make it yours?' Surely you're not going to copy the painting exactly, since you didn't see it with your own eyes. You should add something of your own."

"No, I'm not really an artist. I just know how to copy."

"Rébecca, that's nonsense. You're painting it, aren't you? You're looking at his painting and copying what you see. So pick something of your own to add to the chair there—instead of that ugly pipe—it's not coming out that well anyway, so no harm in taking it out, right? Pick something and copy it, just like you copied the painting. What's the difference?"

There was a big difference, but I couldn't explain it in my bad French. When I was copying a painting I could see the brush strokes, where one color ends and another begins. Vincent van Gogh had already translated the objects in his paintings into two dimensions for me. I'd be lost trying to do that myself. Jessie did it, but she'd been painting for years.

Todd didn't understand that either. When we took the kids back to the vineyards for a hilltop hike later that afternoon, we looked at the terraced hills around us. "You ought to paint this, Beck. If I took a photo, could you do it from that?"

I wished I could. As Ben and Sarah skipped down the path ahead of us, I felt sorely in love with the scene and wished I could keep it on a canvas forever—the rolling hills, the rows of gnarled vines, the men and women pruning as their children played, the picnic table at the bottom of the hill, set up with jugs of wine, cheese, and bread. It was a treat just to walk amidst it. I watched the families hiking together—great-grandparents down to the littlest ones—and felt my heart stretch inside me, swollen and thick.

For nearly a week I'd been a fountain of emotion, sloshing onto anyone who came close enough. I'd see Madame Mallet behind her hedges and think, "I ought to go over there for a kiss," and then I'd do it! We'd only started greeting each other that way two months ago, yet it struck me funny to remember how the custom had once made me cringe. I'd worry about her lips getting too close to mine, and I'd think about her morning breath. But now I only noticed how soft her cheeks were, just like my grandmothers' had been.

I had even found myself giving the double-cheeked kiss to anyone willing at the school gate, and while I'd been happy to do that with my French friends, I'd always thought it was a silly thing for Americans to do—fake, disingenuous. But now I couldn't help myself. I kissed my friends, and I kissed their husbands. It was nice smelling their after-shave, feeling the stubble on their cheek after a day at work.

"Why don't Americans do this back home?" I asked Jessie.

"I've been wondering that for years," she replied.

It deserved a holy card of its own, this holy kissing. I loved the way it drew me close to people I cared about, close enough to smell them, to feel their skin on mine as we both breathed this life together. It felt sacred to me, like a rite, a way to say without talking, "I am glad you're in my life and I thank God for you."

And I was indeed so glad that these people were in my life. I was glad, period. It seemed as if in the last few weeks love and joy had bubbled in me like a fountain. Where had it come from . . . from forgiving myself? Seeing God everywhere and in everyone?

As for drawing the card, how would I do it? A big red pair of kissing lips didn't seem holy enough for a sacred gift, even if it was something people did cheerily, without thinking. I finally settled on drawing Madame Mallet and myself, cheek to cheek.

The tagline would read:

Turn the other cheek and pucker up, because I'm happy to be with you.

2222

OK, so it's a little long. I couldn't help myself.
And the prayer?

> Dear God of bright light streaming, warming everyone it touches, no matter who they are or what mistakes or good they've made, thank you for giving us other people to walk through life together. Help us see you in every one of them, and be brave enough or foolish enough to show them what is in our hearts.

I had gotten so used to kissing my friends that when I saw Stephanie at the school gate on Friday afternoon, I leaned over and kissed her cheek without even thinking about it.

"Oh," she said, waiting for me to finish. "Yes, I'm glad we're friends too, Becky." We hadn't said much more than friendly hellos for a few weeks. I had stopped beating myself up for taking time out from church, and she'd lost interest in the campaign to change my mind. I guess she might have lumped me in with Jessie and the other non-church-going women. At least I was in good company.

"I've been meaning to tell you," she said, "I'm starting a Bible study. I figured you'd want to come since you're missing church. Everyone's bringing their kids, so I'm giving you no excuses." She said it with a wink, but I had the feeling she was serious. "We'd love to have you."

"OK, thanks."

What else could I say? Stephanie was right. There was no reason I couldn't come. But I couldn't sit still reading the Bible on my own couch, let alone surrounded by other people. But if I stayed home, what would people think? I knew the expat community. Bible study would divide it up into two groups: those who went and those who didn't. If I chose not to go, I'd be announcing to my small world that that's not who I am anymore. If I wasn't a church lady, just who would I be?

You'd be God's child, I told myself.

Yes. That's it.

As I pulled into the driveway from school, Madame Mallet was at her gate, waiting on me, hiding something behind her back.

"Rébecca, come here child. I have a present for you."

"A present?"

She nodded and pressed a rock into my palm. On the rock's flat face was a simple painting of a daisy against grass, with sky and sun above. "It's for you: one of my masterpieces."

"Madame Mallet, it's beautiful!"

"Eh, I wouldn't say beautiful. But it's not too ugly," she said. "I didn't copy it from someone else's painting. My little brain knew what a daisy looked like, and I picked one from my garden as a model. So I looked at it. I let my hand remember, and I painted. I made it my painting—not someone else's. You can do that too, my dear."

"Merci," I said, and gave her a kiss, a *bisou*, as thanks. She smiled for a moment and then drew her blue lips into a more comfortable frown.

"Oh, it's not a big deal," she said. "Maybe when I'm dead it will make you rich, just like van Gogh."

I laughed and gave her another holy kiss, just because I wanted to.

Chapter 22

The Sacrament of Pruning

Ella Fitzgerald might have sung about "April in Paris," but she surely wouldn't sing about March. No one would ever write a song about March in France, I thought, cinching the hood of my raincoat against the deluge. If they did, only depressed people would play it, in a dark room, before going out to jump off a bridge.

Sunny, cold February was over, but where was spring? Gone were the ice cold blue sky days, replaced with a constant chilly rain. It'll be here soon, I said to myself, but there were no signs of spring yet, except for the hyacinths, which looked like plastic fakes stuck in the dirt. There was a patch of daffodils beside my driveway, so beaten down by the rain that they seemed to be bending over to throw up.

I'd called in sick for the first meeting of Stephanie's Bible study. I really did have a migraine headache, even if it was brought on by the thought of going. (Sorry God, but it's true.) This time I'd have no excuse.

As I pushed Sam's stroller up the hill after dropping the kids off at school, repeating the mantra "it will be fine, it will be fine," the clouds broke open, pelting me with raindrops. Was it God, saying "Hey, you sunny day lover, the girl who wants to kiss the whole world, let's see how your attitude holds up with a month of dark days—and Bible study."

Sam didn't like the weather either. As I rounded the corner for the long walk up to our parking place, he pulled at the stroller cover and stuck his face out, as if he couldn't breathe in there. "You're going to get wet," I said, and he whined and burrowed back into his seat.

A woman in black sped past us on her motorbike, splashing us. I looked down at my wet clothes. I was wearing black too. No one was wearing the capri pants and Easter egg T-shirts displayed in the windows at Monoprix. It was all black, all day long, and I was tired of it.

By the time we reached the top of the hill I wasn't in the mood to kiss anyone. And what was worse, there was a team of workers wearing les bleus, attacking the tree in front of my car with chain saws. When I had parked there a few minutes earlier, they were setting traffic cones around it.

"I hope they're not going to chop down that tree," Sarah had said, noting how pretty it was, the rounded arc of the treetop, the limbs just starting to bud. Now men in hard hats were hacking off all the new growth, leaving a single tiny stick at the middle of each nub as the chain saws rattled my brain. It looked obscene, as if the branches had morphed into a mob of hands, each giving me the finger. I was wondering why they had to prune like that when someone grabbed my shoulder from behind, startling me.

"Sorry," Jessie yelled above the din of the saw. We kissed each other's wet cheeks.

The chain saws stopped for a half a second and started up again. "Coffee?" Jessie mouthed, pointing to L'Écolier, the rundown café across the street with the dirty awning dripping onto the sidewalk. A man stood underneath it, arms folded, smoking a cigarette and survey-ing the workmen.

I shook my head. The chain saws stopped.

"I can't," I said. "Stephanie just asked me to go with her to Bible study, and I told her that I had to go home to get Sam's diaper bag before it starts."

"Oh, come on. I've got diapers in my car trunk you can have. Let's have a short coffee. It won't take long."

"I can't. I told them I was going home."

"But you don't need to go home. I told you: I'll give you whatever you need. We'll go across the street. They'll be down at Le Lutitia anyway. We'll have a short coffee, and then you can go. They'll never know. Guy told me yesterday he's been wondering where we've been. Just a quick one, please?"

I took the booth where I could see the door, just in case Stepha-nie walked by. By the time Guy (which rhymes with key) brought our coffees to the table, Sam and Abby had fallen asleep in their strollers. We peeled off our coats and sat in the warm smoke.

I glanced at the door.

"Stop worrying, Becky. They wouldn't come in a dive like this." Jessie said. "The smoke would irritate their delicate American lungs."

I laughed. Jessie asked the waiter for a croissant.

"What?" I asked. "No pain au chocolat today?"

"No," she said, digging in her purse for change. "I've given it up for Lent."

"You do Lent?"

"Yeah," Jessie said, glancing up at me. "What? You think I'm such a heathen that I don't do Lent? Everybody does Lent."

"I don't," I said. "It's never been a thing where I go to church. But I do kind of like the idea." Todd had recapped Pastor Joe's sermon about Lent for me, and I was really intrigued by the concept, to prepare for Easter by giving up some attachment, some pleasure, to remind myself of my own weakness as I thought about the struggles Jesus faced. This year I'd had more than enough reminders of my own weakness— enough to hand out to every member of Christ Church—but it still intrigued me. "Maybe I'll try it next year."

Jessie sipped her espresso and unwrapped a tiny chocolate bar from her purse.

"Hey, I thought you were giving up chocolate."

"Oh, yeah," she said and examined it. "Well, it's just a small one. Jesus knows I can't go cold turkey."

"So you're not going to Bible study?"

"Are you kidding?" Jessie said. "Stephanie didn't even ask me. She knows I won't go."

"I don't know about that," I said. "They probably just think you're still in French class every day."

"Maybe. You're going?"

"I guess so."

"Why? You obviously aren't thrilled about it."

"No, I want to go. Well, kind of. The truth is that I'd like to want to go, and I know I should. I've always loved Bible study—I've done it for years. I just don't feel like it right now, but I'm sure it'd be good for me."

"Why?" Jessie asked, staring.

Why? Sometimes Jessie asked the most obvious questions.

"Because God's word is always good for people."

"Then what's the problem?"

"Honestly? The mere idea just makes me want to run in my house and hide. I know it's terrible, but even the thought of someone talking me into going to Bible study irritates me right now. It actually makes me mad!"

Jessie shrugged her shoulders.

"Thanks for the sympathy. You do know this is partly your fault, right? Ever since I started painting I don't want to spend my time doing anything else. Did I tell you I've gridded out my second one? I'm going to do another chair painting to go with the first—the one van Gogh did of Gauguin's chair." I looked around. "There's something else I want to do too. I'll tell you, but you're going to think I've lost my mind."

"I love it already. What?"

"Don't laugh," I said and lowered my voice. "I want to tear the pillows off my couch."

"Tear them off? The one with the green slipcover?"

I nodded. "I've always hated that thing," I said. "And you know what's weirder? I have this crazy feeling that God wants me to do it."

Jessie shrieked. People turned around to look.

"I only bought it because it's the kind my mother-in-law had and I didn't even know what I liked back then. It's got those attached overstuffed pillows, the kind that flop over each other, and they always look smushed. The slipcover never stays in place, and I hate the fabric underneath, the muted colors. I'm pretty sure I could just take a knife and cut those pillows right off. They've got pillows filled with down for a good price at Prix Unique, and I could reupholster the whole thing. I know how to sew, and I have a machine."

"So do it. Go right now and buy the pillows."

"I can't skip out on Bible study just to cut pillows off my couch."

"You have to!"

"I'm not sure that I even know how. I've slip-covered a chair before but never anything that big. If I cut off those pillows, there's no turning back."

"Becky, that's what makes this perfect. Start on it today!"

"But don't you think I should try going to Bible study at least once, just to see if I like it?"

"Why? You just said you didn't want to. If you went, you'd only be doing it for them, right?"

I nodded.

We both drank our coffee. Jessie ran her finger around the edge of her cup in thought. "If you ask me, it's obvious what you need to give up for Lent."

"What?"

"Bible study."

"Jessie!"

"No, I'm serious. It's something you love, right?"

"Usually it is. Usually it's one of my favorite things."

"But it's not good for you right now. You feel like you need it for some reason—to be a good Christian person, whatever. But I wouldn't think ought-to's are good when it comes to faith, right?"

I nodded again.

"So give it up! See what happens."

Could I do that? I'd already given up church for a while. Could I really give up Bible study for Lent? Could I even stop trying to force it at home? Wasn't that sacrilegious? I'd be giving in to my own weakness.

But I wouldn't have to go without it very long. Easter was just four weeks away, and I'd told Todd I'd go back to church then, at least for that day, to see if things had changed.

"Becky, there's a time for everything—a time for studying and a time for living it out." Suddenly Jessie laughed, as if she just thought up a joke. She picked up an imaginary microphone off the table, raised it to her lips, and began to sing—she was singing! Right there in the café! "A time to paint and a time to be born . . . A time to weep, a time to laugh . . ."

What a nut! Singing the Byrds' "Turn! Turn! Turn!" in a crowded café? Everyone was looking at us. Guy came out from behind the bar and was walking our way. What was he to do? Tell her to hush? Throw us out?

"Come on," Jessie said to me like a lounge singer. "You know the words!"

Guy leaned over our table, his brow furrowed. Jessie stopped singing and giggled up at him. Was he going to lecture us about proper behavior at a French café? Jessie looked in his eyes, grasped her microphone again, and softly crooned, "To everything, turn, turn, turn, there is a season, turn, turn, turn."

To my shock, Guy added in his heavily accented English, "And a time to every purpose under 'eaven."

We burst out laughing.

"Bravo!" said one of the teenagers playing pool.

That settled it. It was time to make a change.

But maybe not that instant . . . I was a big chicken and made Jessie stay with me until the coast was clear, until I was sure that Stephanie and the Bible study ladies were on their way back to her house.

As we sat in the booth, sipping our coffees, it occurred to me exactly what my new holy card would be. I'd draw a big pair of pruning shears, big enough to cut the pillows off my couch. Just an hour earlier I'd given shears a bad rap for what they had done to the trees on cours Sablon, but that had been unfair. Cutting off the branches did make the trees ugly for a while, but if they were left alone they'd end up fighting each other for light.

Pruning was a good thing, just like in the vineyards, and it could be good in my living room too. Cutting off those pillows would get me closer to the couch I wanted. At least that's what I hoped. It's possible that I'd ruin the whole thing and have to start all over with a brand new one. If my pruning shears were my latest wonder, they'd need a tagline and a prayer.

The Byrds and Ecclesiastes had already served up the tagline:

To everything there is a season.

Jessie and Guy would be pleased.

And the prayer?

Dear God, master gardener of the true vine, we want to bear fruit. As we try to prune ourselves, removing from our lives things that keep us dead or growing in the wrong direction, guide our hands. Take over the shears when we go too far or cut too little. Make us beautiful in your sight.

Could pruning Bible study from my life for a while be healthy too? Forcing it wasn't working, that was for sure. We finished our coffees and I stepped out into the pouring rain, my heart full of sun, ready to take shears to my couch and set myself free.

Chapter 23
Flying Home with Bells On

As I pulled out a can of spray starch Easter morning, it almost felt like old times. Ben needed his pants pressed, Sarah couldn't find the tights that matched her new dress, Sam had smeared Nutella all over Todd's shoulder, and the special Easter service at Christ Church would start in less than thirty-five minutes.

Today was the first time in three months since I had stepped foot into our little chapel, and I wasn't sure what to expect. At least all the kids would be hyped up on Easter candy, making it easier for me to blend in—that is, if I was still as restless in the pew as I used to be.

It was the big question of the day. Would church be different now that my sabbatical was over? Would I have changed? Sure, my prayers were flowing again and I felt close to God, at least in my natural habitat with nothing to distract me. How would I feel in God's house? When the pump organ started wheezing and the Flames of Hell fired up, would I look at that stained glass Jesus, pray a quick I'm sorry, and run for the door?

At least if we were a couple of minutes late I might have a chance of slipping in unnoticed. I hoped that Stephanie wouldn't make a big deal of my return. Maybe there'd be so many other new faces there that she wouldn't notice me. Even Jessie was planning to come, though I was pretty sure why: the pageantry of Easter and a catered meal at the *auberge* in Orcine? Jessie couldn't resist.

Hopefully she'd bring the girls' coats. After a week of warm weather, winter had rushed in for a last hurrah. As I finished ironing Sarah's dress, Ben stepped out on the balcony to see if he could get by with just a sweater and left the door open.

"Mama," he called, "Listen!"

Listen to what? All I heard was the village church bells, clanging like they always did on Sunday morning.

"They're back!" he yelled. Sarah raced in from her bedroom.

"It's the cloches volant!" she said, and the kids began talking over each other, explaining how the Flying Bells instead of the Easter Bunny bring Easter candy to French children.

"Madame Bioche says that the bells leave their churches on Thursday," Sarah said. "They fly off to Rome to see the pope, taking him everybody's sadness over Jesus being killed on the cross."

"So see? That's why we didn't hear them Friday and Saturday," Ben explained. "But they're back now to celebrate that Jesus isn't dead after all."

There was indeed a lot to celebrate. The resurrection of Jesus was the big event of course, the beautiful celebration of his new life and our eternal closeness to God. But I also had a tiny reason of my own to celebrate, however hesitantly: my first Sunday back at church. I had missed being in God's house, especially after the novelty of staying home wore off. The bells were flying home, and so was I. I hoped I'd be there to stay.

As I walked through the doors to Christ Church Auvergne, I was startled to find it even wilder than before. All the kids were running off a sugar rush. Even Stephanie's zombie-child Jacob was hanging off the side of the pew, slapping people's bottoms as they walked past.

Sam, now sixteen months old, had grown no better at sitting still. He was my same little monkey, climbing around, pulling on my clothing and any sharp objects within reach. At least the activity kept him warm. My feet were turning to ice cubes on the stone floor. All the little girls had winter coats over their Easter dresses, and the Flames of Hell were burning full blast.

As we found our place in a pew, Stephanie left her circle of friends to give me a hug. I looked over her shoulder at the Bible study ladies talking with each other, and I felt a little left out. They were a close-knit group now, not that it surprised me. Bible study always brought people closer. I'd experienced it myself and was happy for them, even though it felt a little strange being on the outside looking in.

"Now that you're back at church again," Stephanie said, "we'd love to have you at Bible study."

"I'll think about that," I said. Even if there was time to explain, she might not understand but that was OK. I wasn't the prodigal daughter, having abandoned my faith, returning to reclaim it once again. I'd left church, not God. I wasn't even sure I was back to stay.

The first part of worship went better than I'd ever expected. The sermon was beautiful, and I'd sat still without a single request for help from toddler Jesus in the window. The only time my mind drifted was during the reading of the scripture, but I could've predicted that. God's Word would return in time. Everything would be back to normal.

Is that what you want, I asked myself . . . to be Church Lady again—or no church at all?

No, it wasn't that. If I was going to be in church, I couldn't be halfhearted. I didn't know another way to be.

When it was time for communion, Father Joe lifted the cloth and poured the wine. I looked at Ben and Sarah and saw yearning on their faces. Was it so important to follow the rules from my childhood? I'd always thought that bending the rules defiled the sacredness of the act. Now I wasn't so sure.

"Mommy," Sarah whispered, "I know why we aren't allowed to do communion, but I still wish we could."

"Yeah," Ben added. "I want to go to God's table too. I wish there was enough for us."

My heart dropped to my stomach.

"Ben, honey, you know that's not it at all," I whispered as Sam climbed onto my lap. "It's just that—"

Sarah interrupted. "It's just that Baptists say you can't sit at the table unless you've been baptized. It's a rule."

"But I believe in Jesus," Ben said.

"I know you do, honey. Here," I said, hoping to distract him with a candy from my purse. If I made exceptions now, what would I tell him the next time? But it felt wrong to keep Ben and Sarah in the pew, watching their friends receive the blessings. Could I break a rule I had always followed, one that came from the church, even if it didn't fit anymore? What was I supposed to do, throw out the rules and invent a whole new way of doing church?

You've changed the rules before, I reminded myself. What about the wine?

I'd found a middle ground on that, but this was a holy ritual. Yes, a ritual, a practice like prayer, giving us the chance to draw near to God. But didn't rituals have prerequisites? The priest himself said that participants had to be baptized. It was clear.

Those kids in line didn't complete any prerequisites, my conscience piped up. Their parents carried them to the font, and the priest dabbed water on their foreheads. God is calling. Your children are calling. Look at them. They're practically begging!

After worship, as we zigzagged our way up to the hillside auberge, I switched back and forth, debating my inner voice.

You don't need those pencil lines anymore. Trust . . .

That only works with paintings, I argued, leaning back in my seat, closing my eyes, trying to listen to my heart. It didn't take much effort; my conscience was right. I couldn't hold back God's blessings from Ben or Sarah or any of us. I refused to. If the rules kept my children from the blessings of God, the rules would have to fall where they may. The question was how to do it. Could I simply choose what I liked and drop what I didn't, as if church was a couch I could choose to dismantle?

But you didn't dismantle it! I argued. You just changed the few parts you couldn't live with anymore. Follow what you know to be true. Make it your faith, not someone else's.

Hadn't Madame Mallet said a similar thing, pressing her rock painting into my palm? "I let my hand remember, and I painted. I made it my painting—not someone else's. You can do that too, my dear."

My faith, my couch, my painting . . . It was sort of the same problem: how to make it mine without wrecking the whole thing.

We parked across from the auberge and as we walked across the street, the village bells clanged loudly in celebration. "Les cloches volant! They're here too!" Sarah said. "Hear the bells, Sammy? It's Easter and we get to have a party. God is alive! Did you know that?"

My little evangelist . . . Sam nodded and laughed and put his hands over his ears.

I would work out how to make my faith my own in time, but Sarah was right. It was time to party that God was alive. It was also time for a new holy card, this time starring les cloches volant, the Flying Bells, who carry away the sadness of the world at Jesus' death and return with sweets, celebrating that God's love always wins. Din Don Din! Clang Clang! I'd draw the bells with feathers on, high in the sky, ringing out the good news.

And the tagline would read:

Listen! Love wins!

What would I write as my prayer?

> Dear God, when we gave you our worst at the cross, you responded with your best. That's how you are, God, and we are so grateful. You take whatever we give you—our prayers, our regret, and our apologies; our songs, our art, and our efforts to be close to you—and you make something beautiful out of them. Give us courage to do that ourselves: to dismantle what in our minds and hearts needs fixing, to prune away the dead wood, to re-create ourselves into the people you want us to be. If we can't see it or we can't do it, God, step in and shape us with your fingers. Then send us into the world like the *cloches volant*, ringing out your joy from wherever we find ourselves. Clang Clang!

Later that afternoon, after the ringing stopped, we'd made it back home and everyone had fallen into a nap in front of the television, I hung my painting of van Gogh's chair the way it was, pipe and all. I'd signed my name at the bottom. Wasn't that enough? So what if Madame Mallet didn't like the pipe? It was my painting, not hers. Besides, the pipe wasn't that bad looking. My Granddaddy Skaggs had smoked a pipe. It could remind me of him.

I stood back and took a full look at it. Why on earth was I stressing? The chair was fantastic! Why couldn't I be happy with it just the way it was? I looked to my fairy godmother clock, half hoping for some reassurance, but she just ticked off the seconds, scolding me with every click. Wasn't it enough that I painted just for the pleasure of it? I'd come so far. I had every right to leave it as it was, satisfied that I had copied it well. It was van Gogh's chair anyway. It didn't have to be mine.

And yet the light beckoned, filtering through my curtains, sending lacy shadows onto the wallpaper of my living room. I opened the doors to the balcony and the room flooded with Easter light, bright, glaring off the painting, making me squint. I shut the doors back, and closed the shutters too. I felt like cocooning. The light was beautiful, but there was something comfortable about the darkness.

Chapter 24
Saint Vincent

Madame Mallet was the only person I'd ever met who'd greet the ringing of church bells with a raised fist.

"Laugh if you want, Rébecca," she said, pointing her pruning shears at me from across the street, "but please explain to me why they must din don din, fill the streets with clatter, and give us all headaches. Easter was over two weeks ago. Enough already! Do they think we're so stupid that we don't know what time it is? Must we be called to weekday mass like dogs?"

I chuckled, dragging our suitcases out to the car. "It's music, Madame Mallet."

"It may be music to you, Rébecca, but to me it's just noise."

I crossed the street for our morning kiss.

"So now you're gallivanting off to Provence," she said, wiping her nose with a handkerchief. "Well, my dear, I'm glad to see France is finally getting into your blood. No more running around with baskets of laundry and that witch's broom of yours. It's a wonder your family has clean clothes to wear, since you now paint your days away—well, when you're not running off on vacation."

I laughed, trying my best to fight off the old urge to apologize and try to look busy and industrious. Madame Mallet had a point. The Easter bells had stopped ringing weeks ago, and we were still in celebration mode—all of France was. We had barely finished our two-week Easter break in April when we were thrown into a long weekend for May Day, and now, just a week later, another one for La Fête de la Victoire.

Madame Mallet had started ticking off a list of sights to see in Arles when the church bells started up again.

"You bells," Madame Mallet yelled out at the ringing, "Why don't you go back to Rome where you belong?"

The din don din might have irritated my neighbor, but it sounded like freedom to me; freedom from the Clermont black—my black winter coat, black sweaters, black pants, black mood; freedom from being stuck indoors; freedom from the April rains, cold wet feet, and the constant tracking in of mud.

I'd laughed on May Day when I showed Todd the traditional bouquet of *muguets* Madame Mallet had given me. "Look," I said, lifting the bell-shaped blossoms with a finger, "It's lily of the valley. Aren't they perfect? Little white liberty bells!"

"Yeah," he said, "liberty to sit around and do nothing. I might as well give up trying to get anything done at work in May. Half the month is vacation, and every other sunny day, the city closes down from one strike or another."

It was true. All over town, people were taking their turns at being *en grève*. The students went first, marching in the sunshine down Avenue Carnot, led by a bongo player in blond dreadlocks and escorted by gendarmes on motorbikes. Next it was the teachers' turn, marching around Place Delille with their banners and signs as children and parents stood on the sidewalk, cheering them on. A few days after that it was time for the doctors to take a turn and then the postmen. One day I even went on a strike of my own, not that I had anything to strike about. I planted myself in a lawn chair underneath the cherry tree, singing quietly the chorus to my new favorite song:

> *Je ne veux pas travailler*
> *Je ne veux pas déjeuner*
> *Je veux seulement oublier*
> *Et puis je fume.*

> I don't want to work.
> I don't want to eat lunch
> I only want to forget
> And then I smoke.

I'd started singing it as a joke, but lately I'd embraced the words—at least the "I don't want to work" part, treasuring every second of my idleness—the singing, the sunshine, the birds landing on the branches above me, sending the blossoms falling like snow. There were blessings, blessings, everywhere. And to top it all off? A few more days of les vacances.

When Todd said, "Let's go see Provence," I nearly knocked him down with a hug. We'd never been to southern France, the land of van Gogh's *Starry Night*, his haystacks and chairs. Everyone gushed about the charm of Provence, the *bouillabaisse* and the *ratatouille*, the landscapes and the light. My French friends gave me lists of things to see in and around Arles: the Church of St. Trophime, the arena, Le Pont du Château.

On the way out the door I added Jessie's book of paintings to my tote bag, thinking I'd browse through it at the hotel after the kids went to bed and pick out painting number three, maybe a gift for my mom or my sister-in-law. But when the kids got sleepy in the car after lunch I started flipping through the paintings. I'd never noticed they were arranged chronologically before, illustrating van Gogh's life story. I started reading about his life. It shocked me.

Vincent van Gogh had chained himself to the church too! Before he'd dedicated his life's work to painting, he'd tried to be a preacher and evangelist like his father. He'd even given away all his things to the poor, to more closely identify with them. Vincent was also a copier. He'd taught himself to paint by copying the masters, and at times would get so frustrated with his mistakes that he'd swear off painting forever.

As we drove south into the sun, I made my way through the book, watching van Gogh's work turn from the somber colors of peasant life in Holland to the acidic colors of Provence. Even in his mental illness—or maybe because of it—he stepped away from the masters' work and walked out on a limb of his own making, creating a unique style to express what he found holy. I looked at the wide, aggressive brush strokes in *Wheat Field with Crows* and could feel his passion in the thick spackled paint.

I read excerpts from his letters to his brother Theo, in which he described Jesus as "the supreme artist, more of an artist than all others, disdaining marble and clay and color, working in the living flesh."

Yes! This was exactly what I felt as I wandered in my wilderness away from church. God was working in the living flesh! As van Gogh painted the people he found in Provence—the postmen, barkeeps, and prostitutes—he painted God inside of them. I could see it in all those holy nobodies, in Pale Lady, in Madame Mallet and the weasel man, in Madame Pink Suit and Saint Clotilde, in the crying singer and Monsieur Desnoyer. They were lining up in my brain, as if waiting for me to put them somewhere—not on a continuum of bad to good, but circling around me, lingering.

The sun blazed through my car window onto the pages, making me yawn. We'd soon see it all, the fields where van Gogh set up his easel and paints, the streets of Arles, the light and the mountains. Todd put in a Francis Cabrel CD, "*Samedi Soir sur la Terre*," and I closed the book on my lap. The mellow guitar and the warm sun cradled me, and I closed my eyes for a moment.

Vincent met me in a sleepy half-dream, sitting down beside me on our frumpy old couch, the way it looked before I'd recovered it. I was the old me, the one before I'd found my fairy godmother clock, before France had oozed into my blood. Jessie's book was open on my lap.

"Perfection has always eluded me," Vincent said, holding the clay pot I'd made as a child in second grade at school. That pot had always made me sad. We were supposed to coil snakes of clay around and around to form the sides, but mine came out lumpy and uneven. In tears I had sneaked it into the bathroom where I rolled it out on the floor and then drew rope lines around it with a pencil tip. I still felt sorry for my little second grade perfectionist self, crouched in the bathroom, cheating to make my pot perfect. But back to van Gogh . . .

I looked at the pot in his hands, at the pencil lines I'd made in the clay, at the paint under his fingernails. He nodded at Jessie's book, at his self-portrait on the page. "I did that one in Paris, when I first moved there. See the unsure eyes? I was just coming out of the dark then."

Todd nudged my arm, rousing me out of my half-sleep, whispering, "Beck, you've got to see this."

I squinted against the bright light and adjusted my eyes. We had driven into one of van Gogh's paintings! Blackish cedars cut the fields of wheat into squares. There were purple hills in the distance and clouds, churning and spinning clouds, just like the ones Vincent had painted.

And the light! It was true. The light was different here, as if a film had peeled back from the windshield. Everything sparkled, vibrated in the light—the sky above us, the fields, the poplar trees bordering both sides of the two-lane road, the rippling roof on the shed in the distance.

I flipped through the book and found a painting with a similar landscape. "Kids, look at this!"

We spent the entire weekend that way, passing the book from me to the children to Todd as we wandered around Arles, following the footsteps of Saint Vincent van Gogh. The fields of poppies, the vineyards bushy and green, the wildflowers blooming in a ditch by the side of the road, it all felt like God reaching out to me . . . God growing in the vines up to me. How could we not notice it, feel it? No wonder van Gogh had painted here.

We drove around the surrounding countryside, trying to match landscapes and sheds to the ones in his paintings, breathing in the warm air, smelling the grass and listening to the bees and birds where we stopped by the side of the road.

Sarah flipped to the painting *Les Alyscamps, allée à Arles.* "I want to go there," she said.

"No problem," said Todd, and we headed back to the outskirts of town. More than a hundred years ago, when van Gogh had done his series of paintings at the Roman necropolis on the edge of Arles, the leaves were orange and yellow. Now they were green with spring, but the tombs and the trees looked the same. Ben and Sarah took turns using the paintings as treasure maps, searching out the exact spot where he'd put his easel, matching the village walls and chimneys.

"You know what we ought to do?" Todd said, as we climbed back into the car. "Find a museum and see one of those paintings up close . . . a real work of van Gogh, with his very own brush strokes." The kids thought it was a great idea, the perfect finish to our vacation: to see the paint that had smeared on his fingers, a canvas he'd actually wedged under his arm as he lugged his easel, brushes, and paints into a wheat field or up a hillside or onto a cobblestone street.

An hour later we had to face facts. In all of Arles, where van Gogh painted some of his best known works—*Café Terrace on the Place du Forum, Peach Tree in Blossom, The Postman*—not a single one was on display.

"But these paintings are all inspired by van Gogh," the lady at the Fondation Vincent van Gogh insisted, waving us in. We said a polite merci and kept walking. Sarah sighed loudly and Ben said, "I think I might feel better with some ice cream."

After a stop at a sunny café, Todd and Ben took Sam back to the hotel for a nap and Sarah and I went window shopping.

"Mama, look! It's a store full of santons! See? There's a whole crèche, just like at Orcival!" Of course! We were in the heart of Provence, where all of France's crèches had come from. The store had thousands, of every imaginable size and kind. There were tiny terra cotta ones with painted-on clothes, and larger ones, like dolls, dressed in Provencal fabrics and carrying items of all possible professions—baskets of lavender, tatted lace, cobbler's benches, and chimney brushes.

"Oh, let's get one, please? We could put it with our nativity set. See?" she said, picking up a lady selling lavender and walking her through the air. "She could be coming to visit Baby Jesus."

"Maybe," I said, and she clapped her hands and surveyed the store.

"They're all so cool. I wish the people at our old church could see them. They'd want to make santons a brand new Baptist ritual."

"I think they're great too. But honey, our church doesn't really have rituals."

Sarah laughed, as if I were joking.

"Yes they do. I told my Sunday School class all about them. You know, how we pass the little crackers and juice—but only the baptized are allowed—everybody else has to watch, no matter how much they love God or want to do it. And I told them how the minister always invites people at the end to join the church or become a Christian, and how we baptize people in the big tub of water, just like Jesus was baptized. Everybody thought it was funny that the preacher wears hip waders so his pants don't get wet. All that stuff."

Sarah stopped and leaned over a display. "Hey look at that one. It looks like van Gogh!" The santon had a red beard and a painter's smock, a palate and brush in hand. "And look, Mommy, there's the chef from Thanksgiving!"

It did look like Monsieur Desnoyer with his toque and wooly eyebrows. Suddenly my film peeled back for a moment of clarity. This is where they all belonged—Pale Lady, Madame Pink Suit, Monsieur Desnoyer, the crying man. They were all my patron saints, my holy nobodies, ragtag and altogether human, making their way to the Son of God.

"Oh, when the saints go marching in, oh, when the saints go marching in. . . . Lord, how I want to be in that number . . ."

I could step in faith and get in line behind them, firm in the confidence that God was loving me forward on the path, and that the rituals I'd once feared—the Eucharist, the creeds and repeated prayers, even the candles and incense and the cross draped over me—were living guide wires to God, helping me to find my way in the sun and the darkness.

"Mom?" Sarah said, breaking into my thoughts, "I'm glad they didn't put a bandage on his ear."

"Hmm?"

"A bandage, on the van Gogh santon . . . I'm glad they didn't put one on him."

I nodded. Vincent van Gogh was so much more than his weaknesses and his darkest hours. He deserved his own place on a saint card. I'd put him there, minus the bandage on his ear. I'd copy the self-portrait he did in Arles. Vincent wouldn't mind. He was a copier too.

And the tagline?

Serving the supreme artist who works in the living flesh

The prayer came easily:

Dear God, thank you for coming to us as Jesus, the artist above all others, who worked—and still works—in living flesh. Help us spend our lives among others, finding him every place we go, striving to match our footsteps and actions to his. We won't be able to do it, Lord, but there will be joy in the trying. Peel away the film before our eyes so that in your true light, Lord, vibrating with love, we can see people as you see them, as your cherished children.

As we walked back to the hotel, I wondered if we could make it home in time for church on Sunday. There was something I needed to do.

Chapter 25
Five for Supper

As I stepped into an oval of sunlight inching up the central aisle of Christ Church Auvergne, the hair stood up on the nape of my neck. The chapel glowed, as if the evening light had followed me back from Provence and was determined to get in, seeping through every crack and crevice of the building, pressing against the stained glass, giving highlights to Boy Jesus' curls.

Anyone watching would have thought that I was scanning the pews for a good place to sit, not giving myself a pre-Eucharist pep talk. You can do it, I coached myself. The God of the Wilderness had opened my eyes. I was ready for the next step—ready, but jumpy.

I hadn't been this excited about going to church since our first visit in September, when I assumed church would continue to be the stable rock of my life that it had always been. It'd be almost funny if it hadn't shaken me so. But today was my chance to start over again, to follow the example of Saint Vincent van Gogh. I'd learned from the masters, and my foundation was strong. It was time to step out on a limb.

But wasn't van Gogh mentally ill?

I ignored that old voice from my past, trying to protect me from change. I wouldn't quit now, not after I'd come so far.

We greeted our friends in the pews. I felt sorry that I'd been so guarded around them. Weren't they just like me, wanting to connect with God, hoping for friendship and acceptance? Stephanie waved to me from the other side of the aisle, giving me the thumbs-up sign. Months ago I might have jumped to the conclusion that the gesture was only a nonverbal "Hey, heathen, glad you finally showed up." But I could see she was happy that I was here. So was I.

I settled Sam in the pew between me and Ben. Theresa was placing the bread on the altar, covering it with a starched white cloth. In a matter of minutes I'd toss away the rules I'd attached to that bread for all of my thirty-five years, laws I'd nearly worshipped. I'd walk my non-baptized children up to the table and let Father Joe give them the bread. I hadn't discussed this with Todd, but I knew he'd agree.

We'd argued for years over this. Todd hadn't seen the point of making them wait, pointing out that our own minister at First Baptist had opened communion to anyone who'd find it meaningful. Besides, we'd had the children dedicated to God in a service much like infant baptism in other churches, minus the water. "You're just being legalistic," he'd said. The comment stung, but I'd held to my convictions.

I didn't want to admit it, but secretly I knew the requirement of baptism before communion would serve as a bribe: get baptized first, kids, and then we'll let you eat with us. This seemed weird now, requiring one ritual for the participation in another. Hadn't I distrusted rituals in the first place?

"Guess what I just did!" Sarah said, scooting into the pew. "You're going to like this, Mommy. I finally told Emily that she and Joseph have got to stop bugging me and Ben to get in line with them during communion!"

"You did?"

Sarah nodded. "I explained everything. I said, 'Baptists take their rules seriously, and the rule says no communion until after you're baptized.' She didn't know we'd never been baptized—see, she was baptized as a little baby. A baby! Before she could even know whether she loved God or not!"

"About that, Sarah," I said, "I've been thinking and I . . ."

Everyone stood as the pump organ wheezed out the opening strains of "My Faith Looks Up to Thee."

Now what would I do?

By the time Father Joe began his sermon, I'd argued with myself through two scripture readings and three hymns, asking for guidance during the prayers. I tried to concentrate on his words, but my eyes kept drifting off to the table behind him, to the chalice, the pitcher, and the bread, all covered with cloths to keep them holy, free from impurity.

When Father Joe finally finished and everyone stood to shake hands and pass the peace, my heart raced to a full gallop. Communion was next. The people in the first two pews filed into the aisle and I looked to Toddler Jesus, his arms outstretched.

A girl at the front started playing a hymn on a flute and Todd stretched his arm around me, caressing my shoulder. Boy Jesus' eyes looked sympathetic, as if he felt for me: Look at you, so tied to your rules, your little checklist for earning my love.

Meanwhile, Jesus stood at the door, waving everybody in for free.

It was almost our turn.

If it was wrong, I'd have to trust God to show me. I caught Todd's eye, raised my eyebrows in a question, and nodded from the table to the kids.

"What?" Todd whispered. The kids stared at me.

When they looked away I tried again, nodding from the table to the kids.

"Oh," Todd mouthed, "OK."

Emily and Joseph walked by our pew, making a point to look in the other direction. Sarah patted my knee. "See?" she said. "They finally got the message."

"Sarah, I've been wrong about communion."

"No, you haven't."

"Yes. I have."

I nudged Ben. "Would you two like to come up with us for the bread?"

A corner of Ben's lip curled up. He nodded.

"Are you sure?" Sarah whispered. "What about the rules?"

"I'm putting the rules aside. We've spent your whole lives teaching you about Jesus. If you want to do it, I think God would want you there."

"Yes!" Ben said as he hustled out of the pew before I could change my mind.

Would I feel guilty later for lifting the velvet rope, sneaking them in without permission? Maybe . . . But as I watched them stand in line, practically bursting with joy to be counted among God's people, I was sorry I'd waited so long. It might not be right for everyone, but it was right for me.

Ben cupped his hands the way he'd seen the other boys do, pressing his lips together as he waited, squeezing out his grin into something more serious as Father Joe handed him his morsel of bread. Sarah bowed her head, took the bread, and chewed reverently, and then walked leisurely back to the pew, as if it was something she did every Sunday. Sam even quieted himself in Todd's arms, opening his mouth like a baby bird as Todd fed him.

As Ben and Sarah watched the others finish, they didn't slump or sigh or beg for gum. They sat tall in the pew, alert, and I felt so glad for them. We'd shared the sacred treasure—one I couldn't bear to keep to myself.

The bread and the wine, this holy supper symbolizing the body and blood of Christ, certainly deserved a holy card of its own. I would draw it on the altar table: the bread, broken and ready to serve from its platter, the wine in its pottery chalice, ready to be shared. The starched white cloths would be gone. I didn't want anything blocking the way of the bread and the wine for anyone who wanted it.

The tagline?

The bread of life and the cup of salvation. Take, eat, drink all of it.

The prayer came before I could even bow my head:

God, who offers us a taste of yourself, we're so hungry for you. We need you in our lives, nourishing us, giving us your divine energy to follow in your way. None of us have earned this meal. We open our mouths like baby birds, and you feed us yourself out of your own hands. Thank you that there's always enough for everyone, no matter who we are or what we have or haven't done.

I was wrong about the whole Eucharist thing—dismissing the fancy name for the Lord's Supper as a way to appear intellectual. No, the Eucharist deserved the name. It was extraordinary, really, our community of Christians—a line of wayward saints, each of us chipped or broken in some sort of hidden way, none of us really worthy or without sin—all approaching the table, making Jesus a physical part of us, under God's roof.

As we stood to sing "Amazing Grace," the tears came again.

"I once was lost, but now am found; was blind, but now I see."

Thank you, Sweet Lord, for long-lost sight.

Monday morning was glorious. We rolled down the windows on the way to school just to smell the lilac trees and the fresh baked bread, to hear the birds and the sounds of the city. Jessie asked me to go to coffee, but I'd hurried home instead. After the beautiful service Sunday night I was inspired to take one last step. I'd accepted grace from God. Now could I give it to myself?

It was time to paint over the pipe.

I took the painting of van Gogh's chair off the wall, propped it against the balcony rail in the sun, and brought some toys out for Sam to play with beside me. I'd just brought out my brushes when Madame Mallet waved from her bedroom window. She reappeared on her balcony, a book in hand. "So did you find the ghost of your crazy Dutch boyfriend?"

"No," I laughed, "Well, sort of."

She gave me a funny look and then shrugged her shoulders. "You're painting again?"

I nodded.

"Well you never showed me your finished chair. I still hate that pipe, just so you know."

"I know."

"You can choose something much better than a pipe. And you should do it before you start something new."

"Yes, you're right, Madame Mallet."

What would I put in the chair, I wondered. I knew what the old me would choose: the silver cross I'd found at the flea market or the Bible from my childhood.

No. I loved those things, but God loved more about me than just that part of my life.

I stepped around Sam and walked into the house for inspiration. There was the laundry I'd stacked from last night, my grandmother's handkerchief folded neatly on top. I could put that on the chair. What else?

The clock . . . maybe fit it in the background? No, she seemed to say, swinging her pendulum at me. No, this is about you, not me. I only mark the time.

Sam's rabbit, his doudou, was on the side table by the couch, along with the pincushion I'd used in finishing the last steps of my upholstery. Perfect. These things would show the heart of who I am: a woman, a mother, a creator and mender of people and things. It was who I came from, who I was happy to be.

Perhaps I'd finally discovered my purpose in France, the grand mission I'd hoped for ever since we boarded the plane. How funny that my year of searching could be distilled into one simple question: What would I paint on van Gogh's chair? I didn't need a Bible to prove my love or a diploma or volunteer badge to prove I was worthy. I loved God and God loved me whether I went to church or not. I didn't need to prove anything at all.

I unfolded the handkerchief, wadded it as if it had come out of my pocket, and set it on the edge of the chair next to the painting, studying its colors in the light. As the sun turned the haphazard folds into shadows, I picked up my brush. How on earth would I paint that?

You can do it. Just look.

I focused my eyes on the cloth, the individual little stitches of the blue flowers around the edge, the rolled hem.

You're thinking again. Stop it.

I closed my eyes and opened them slowly, trying just to let the colors meet my eyes, not interpret the shadow or see the work or process of it. Finally, the shadow became blue-gray with dabs of charcoal, the edge, silver in the glint of light. As my heart fluttered I picked up the brush, dipped it in black and white on my palate, and swirled the colors into the gray of a pigeon's wing. I steadied my brush, leaned toward the canvas, and slowly stepped out on a limb.

Chapter 26

The Saint in the Mirror,
Wet Behind the Ears

I never thought I'd see an actual mutiny until I spent eight hours at Charles de Gaulle airport, waiting to catch a flight to Atlanta for our three-week summer vacation in the States. When they announced that our flight had been delayed yet again, the Americans started scaring me, throwing down their backpacks and copies of the *Herald Tribune*, ranting to each other.

Todd and I looked at each other and sighed. At least the kids were entertained. Sam was having a fine time tearing up a little notepad, page by page, and Ben and Sarah were unnaturally quiet, fascinated by the circle of American teenagers sprawled out a couple of yards away, whining about how tired they were—and hot. Couldn't a civilized country like France have decent air conditioning? The kids pulled off jackets and sweaters, passed around a communal bag of pains au chocolat, and went back to the rollicking stories of exchanges they'd had with waiters in cafés all over Paris. Apparently it was hilarious.

I watched my mesmerized children. Just a year ago they'd hardly noticed the American kids on the plane camping out by the bathrooms, keeping us awake with their constant chatter. The French, however, had kept them spellbound, as beautiful words twirled out of their mouths.

I'd bought a little bit of France to take back to almost everyone: sachets of lavender, bottles of *herbes de provence,* and lots and lots of chocolate. A full week before our trip I'd lugged the suitcases out of the cave—now crowded with cases of cidre and wine—and started packing. We'd finished off the cidre in the fridge, taken Katie the cat to a kennel in the countryside, and let our fairy godmother clock wind her way down, pausing time until our return.

Before we'd fastened the shutters and turned off the lights, I took the eggs and milk across the street to Madame Mallet. We kissed each other au revoir, and she promised to keep an eye on things. I knew she would. If I'd learned anything in our year together, it was that she was an expert at keeping watch.

As the plane took off, we said goodbye to Clermont and watched it get smaller and smaller beneath us. It felt as if we were leaving home. I handed Sam his doudou, the rabbit now immortalized on a painting above my reupholstered couch.

How Sammy had changed. He was a toddler now, running every-where in his little red shoes, my constant sidekick, my happy accomplice, mimicking Madame Mallet on the balcony as she led them in calisthen-ics just for her own amusement.

I looked across the aisle at Ben and Sarah peering out the window at the clouds. Ben had made it through French first grade, making friends with everyone in his class, begging to stay at school during lunch so as not to miss the soccer games. This little wild boy of mine had become suddenly focused, studying for his dictées, practicing his poesies.

Sarah was growing up too. Just two weeks earlier she'd told me she wanted to be baptized. "Now that I'm going to the table like everybody else, I want to make it official that I'm God's child too, not just yours and Daddy's."

"Father Joe could probably baptize you here," I said, trying my best to look enthusiastic.

"What, get sprinkled?"

I nodded.

"No way! I want to go all the way under—like we do back at First Baptist."

I have to admit it: I sighed with happiness.

Now, as we waited, it was all arranged. We'd go back to Greer for a few days to visit, to see our friends and the folks at church, and Sarah would make her public profession of faith in a weekday baptismal service just for her.

As the trip neared, Sarah asked me over and over to tell her the story of my baptism. I described the entire event, how our minister, Doctor Lawrence, had come to my house and how we practiced on the shag carpet in our den. "I held onto his arm like this," I said, "and he dipped me back, as if we were dancing."

"What did it feel like?"

"The water was warm, and the tile felt cold on my feet. And you know what else? I can still remember the words Doctor Lawrence said: 'Rebecca Diane Skaggs, upon your profession of faith in Jesus Christ and in obedience to his command, I baptize you, my sister, in the name of the Father and the Son and the Holy Ghost.' Then he dipped me into the water, and it was done."

"But I mean, how did it feel inside?" Sarah asked.

"Calm," I said. "Like a tomb. And you know what I did when I was under the water? I opened my eyes, just in case I could see God."

Sarah smiled and then looked up at me, suddenly serious. "You didn't, did you?"

"No. All I saw was the white of the gown as it drifted toward my face. And then he pulled me up, and I rubbed my eyes, and that was it. That was the beginning."

"And then you were one of them," Sarah said. "Mama Judy and Granddaddy had to let you do communion then, right? You were an official one of the saints."

"Yes, I guess so."

It made me laugh to think that I had come to France afraid that I might backslide, hoping that my spiritual life might merely hover steady. I had waded into the baptismal waters of France completely unaware, and God had dipped me back into the very wilderness that I needed, my own personal upside-down Lent, drenching me in bliss. All the things I'd thought I had to have in my life had fallen away—my work, my comfortable place in church, my ability to express myself or feel accomplished.

And as I stepped away from the safety of the pews and into his world, floundering in the water, God's choir of holy nobodies had passed me from one to another, buoying me up, opening my eyes to a much bigger God than I had ever imagined, a God who would not be trapped within hymns, verses, stained glass, or whatever tradition deemed good or acceptable.

One by one the saints revealed to me the wildness of God's love until I began to recognize it for myself, to see it hiding in the darkness as well as in the light. God's grace had soaked me to the core, and I emerged from the waters just like before, rubbing my eyes, staggering into a new life.

The restrooms at the Charles de Gaulle airport in Paris were not a good place for toddlers, given their grabby hands and tendency to suck on things. The boys took the first turn as Sarah and I waited outside *les toilettes* with Sam. The door had just closed behind them when a lady approached us, cigarette in hand, pushing a runny-nosed little boy in a stroller.

"Excuse me," she said in French. "I'm sorry to bother you, but are you going to be here for a couple of minutes?"

"Yes."

"Would you mind watching the baby while I go to the bathroom?"

"No problem. Go ahead."

Sarah knelt in front of the little boy as Sam lunged forward, trying to give him a full body hug. I pulled Sam up on my hip and smiled at the little guy. A head cold was the last thing we needed.

"Bonjour, toi!" Sarah said and as he grinned, the drippy trail from his nose neared his mouth. I found a Kleenex in my purse and wiped his nose as Sarah picked up his doudou, a little orange monkey, and made it dance and talk to him in French.

I looked around for his mommy and noticed a pair of white-haired ladies watching her from a few yards away. The fanny packs and tennis shoes were a giveaway: they were definitely American. I didn't blame them for watching Sarah. She was being awfully sweet, our own version of Clotilde on the train.

Todd and Ben came out and took Sam back to our seats, leaving us with the boy in the stroller. Where was the mother? The lines were probably long. Finally she walked out of the restroom, looping her scarf back around her neck.

"Thank you so much," she said. "You're American, aren't you?"

I nodded.

"I thought so. I could tell by your accent."

"I know. Sorry," I laughed.

"No, it's charming!" She went on to explain that she was from Martinique and had brought her son to visit her mother in Paris for the first time. Now they were heading home.

As we talked, I could feel the ladies still watching us. What were they looking at? I felt the belt of my skirt as we said our goodbyes. Was I zipped?

As Sarah and I walked into the restroom, the women followed in after us. Did they want something?

A flight attendant stood at the sink, in front of a stall with the door ajar.

"*C'est libre?* (It's free?)" Sarah asked.

"*Oui*," she answered, walking out the door.

"*Allez-y* (Go ahead)," I said to Sarah without thinking. She giggled at me for speaking French.

This was uncomfortable, the American women standing behind me, silent. I threw the Kleenex away and washed my hands.

"These French," whispered one lady to the other. "I'll miss their *joie de vivre*. You can just tell it by looking at them. Did you notice her skin?"

"Shh," the other woman said. "I think most of them speak English and just won't admit it. But since you mentioned it, I want her legs."

Was that what they'd been staring at? I'd noticed the Martinique lady's flowery skirt, but I hadn't noticed her legs.

"It's because they walk everywhere. You know, I wish I'd shopped for clothes while we were here. I like that skirt. Of course I couldn't wear pink. It's not my color."

Pink? She was in blue, not pink. I was the one wearing pink. I looked back at them in the mirror, and it dawned on me. They were staring at me! My skirt, my legs . . . They think I'm French! This was hilarious! Only someone who spoke no French whatsoever would hear me speak and think I was a native. I bit my lip to keep from laughing.

Sarah came out, and I tried to stifle my secret joke, afraid that I'd look at her and burst into laughter. She finished washing her hands, and I leaned over to turn off the water for her. My purse fell forward, skimming the side of the sink. I tossed it back over my shoulder, and caught a glimpse of someone in the mirror looking back at me. It was the lady in the pink suit, but it was me, in my skirt and sandals, my white shirt unbuttoned down to there. I looked at my skin, glowing and tanned from walks in the sun, my eyes bright from delicious sleep.

I knew I was far, far away from displaying the elegance of Madame Pink Suit with her basket full of roses and the easy way she moved, but I suppose Sarah was right. I was one of the saints as we all could be, full of brokenness and imperfection, yet beautiful in my own unique way, treasured by God.

Drawing myself on a saint card was going a little too far to be comfortable. Besides, a simple sketch couldn't show what made me happiest of all, how God had opened my eyes and stretched my heart this year, helping me see glimpses of him in a stack full of saints and holy wonders, maybe even catch sight of him moving in myself, flaws and all. I settled on sketching out a mirror. It made sense to me, reflecting the image of anyone willing to look into it, willing to see the broken, treasured child whom God holds dear. But what about the prayer?

Back in the waiting area everyone was gathering their things and standing up, moving in one huge mass toward the doors.

"It's time?" I asked Todd.

"No," he said, opening up the newspaper. "Everybody's just antsy. But our plane finally got here. It'll be at least another half hour before everybody's out and they finish cleaning it."

I walked to the window and watched the passengers exiting the plane onto the portable stairway, squinting into the sun and clutching their passports, eager to step into a whole new world.

I envisioned a tagline as I pointed my prayer their way:

Le Répas est prêt.
The feast is ready.
Take, eat, and fear not.

God, who knit us together in our mothers' wombs, thank you for loving us just as we are. As we each look into the mirror, help us see the broken, treasured child whom you hold dear. Set us each day on a holy treasure hunt, watching for your signs and wonders in every corner, for saints in each face, for your fingerprints in ordinary things. And as we make our way back to church, because we can't help but long to praise you, teach us your way of love. Then shoo us out into the world, the table set with your feast. Make us ready, Lord, to take and eat and fear not. Amen.

CPSIA information can be obtained
at www.ICGtesting.com
Printed in the USA
BVHW04s1434110718
521390BV00027B/1081/P